AF521675

POCKET ART GUIDES

RELIEF
Painting

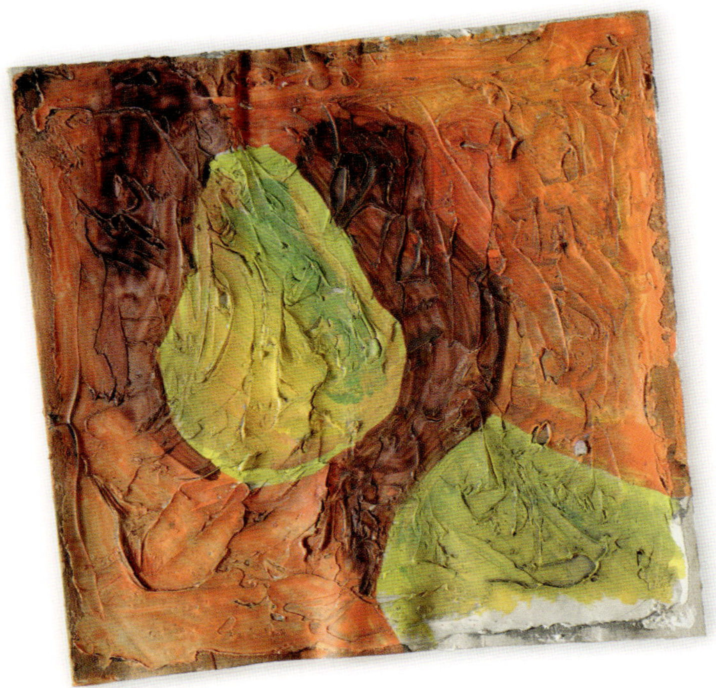

BARRON'S

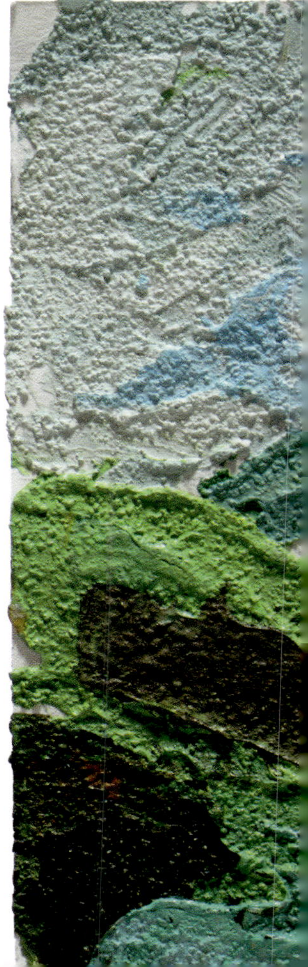

First English editIon for the United States and Canada
published in 2012 by Barron's Educational Series, Inc.

Published by ParramonPaidotribo, S.L., Badalona, Spain.
Original title of the book in Spanish: *La pintura en relieve*
Text: Gabriel Martín Roig
Exercises: Gabriel Martín and Óscar Sanchís
Photography: Estudi Nos & Soto

All inquiries should be addressed to:
Barron's Educational Series, Inc.
250 Wireless Boulevard
Hauppauge, NY 11788
www.barronseduc.com

ISBN: 978-0-7641-6534-4

Library of Congress Control Number: 2011943023

Printed in China
9 8 7 6 5 4 3 2 1

POCKET ART GUIDES

RELIEF
Painting

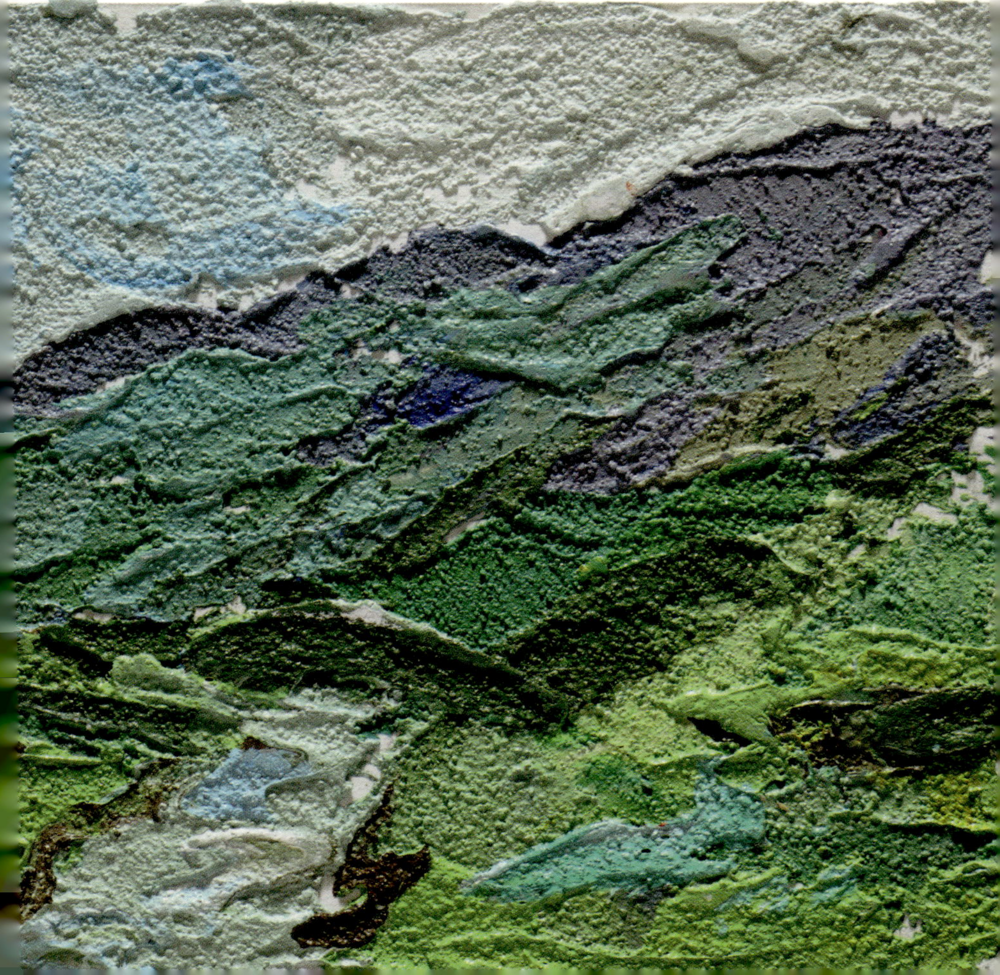

Contents

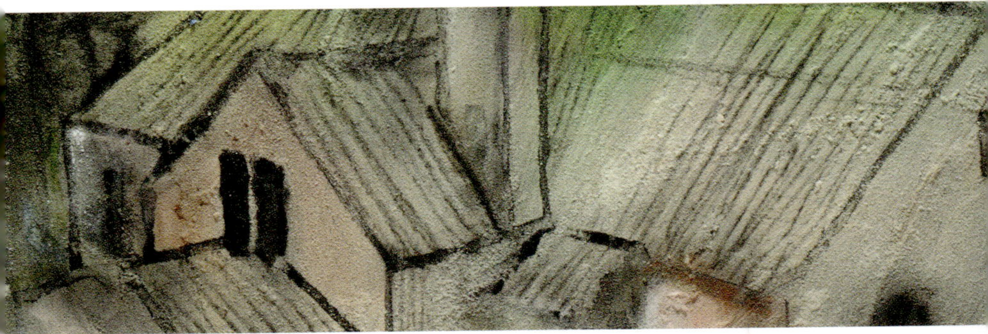

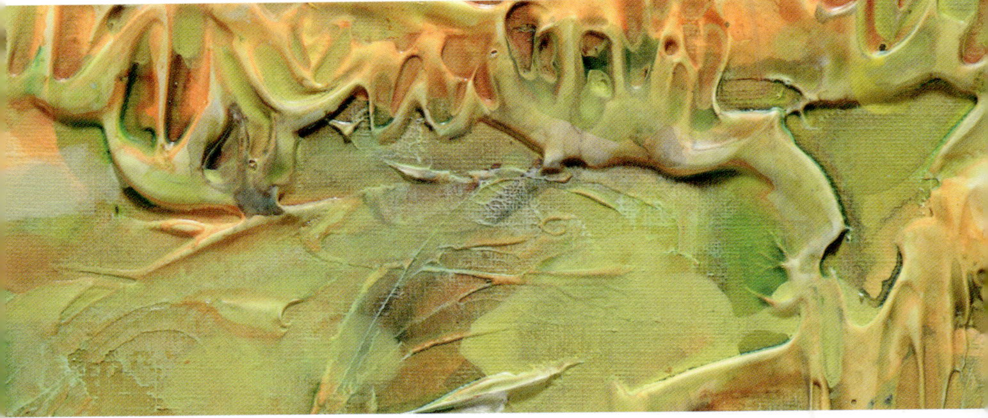

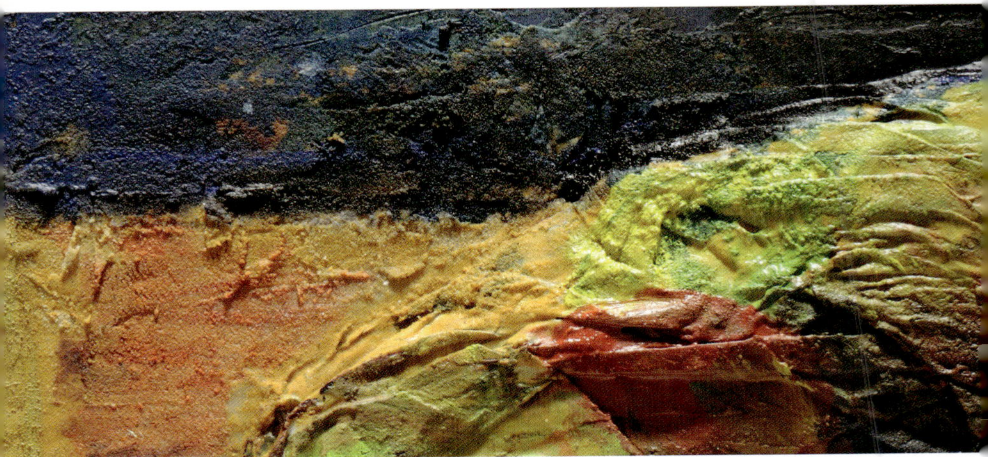

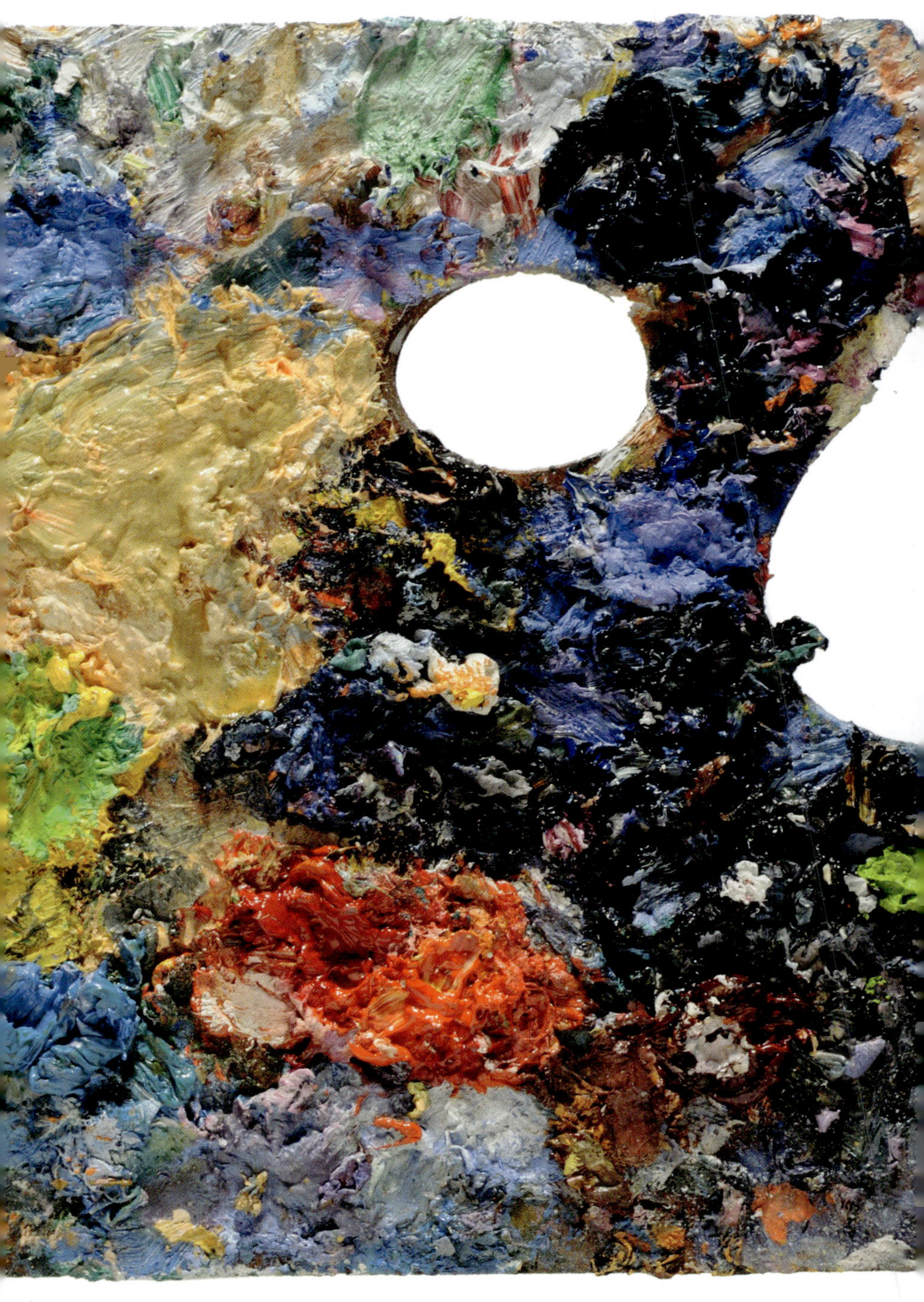

Texture, Adding a Differentiating Quality

Texture is an accumulation of forms or raised materials that can be perceived as variations and irregularities on the surface of a painting. The thickness and relief of the paint is emphasized. Texture is utilized to add graphic richness and a tactile sense of color. Preparing the texture is a very important aspect of a semiabstract, abstract, or informal interpretation of any subject. The point of adding texture to the paint is to create new feelings by altering one's final perception of the colors—as if the artist were trying to challenge the viewer's common sense, or create confusion with new effects added to the purely chromatic ones. Relief effects are, therefore, added to paintings to give them a fresh personality and to distinguish them from more traditional works.

Textures can be layered over each other as if they were planes on the picture, only now you are not just working with color, but also with filler. It is like superimposing another language on the painting that will coexist with the purely chromatic one. But ultimately, color and texture should be perceived as a single entity. No attempt should be made to disassociate them since the perception of textured paint is optical and not tactile. Despite what many people think, the information is not meant to be tactile; it is not necessary to touch the surface of a painting to know what texture it has. This information connects to our vision because it is perceived when the painting is illuminated, affecting the values of the reflected light and casting the shadows caused by the high relief.

If an artist has never painted with textures, he or she will find that relief painting will open doors to new possibilities. Textures, when used well, offer a wide range of expressive effects, and also impart a very modern "now" look. Surprisingly, relief painting can be economical, because combining paint with fillers, gels, and modeling pastes of all kinds give it added viscosity and density while using less of it. At the same time the colors seem to be richer and more varied. In this book, artists interested in experimenting with textures will find helpful explanations of the techniques for creating relief on painted surfaces. To put them into practice, it is necessary to become familiar with the characteristics of all the available materials and approaches first: the supports, the models, the materials, and the ways of applying relief to a surface.

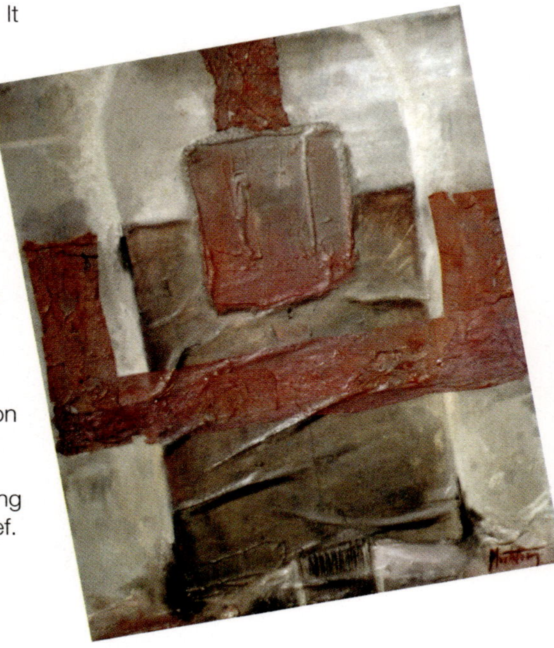

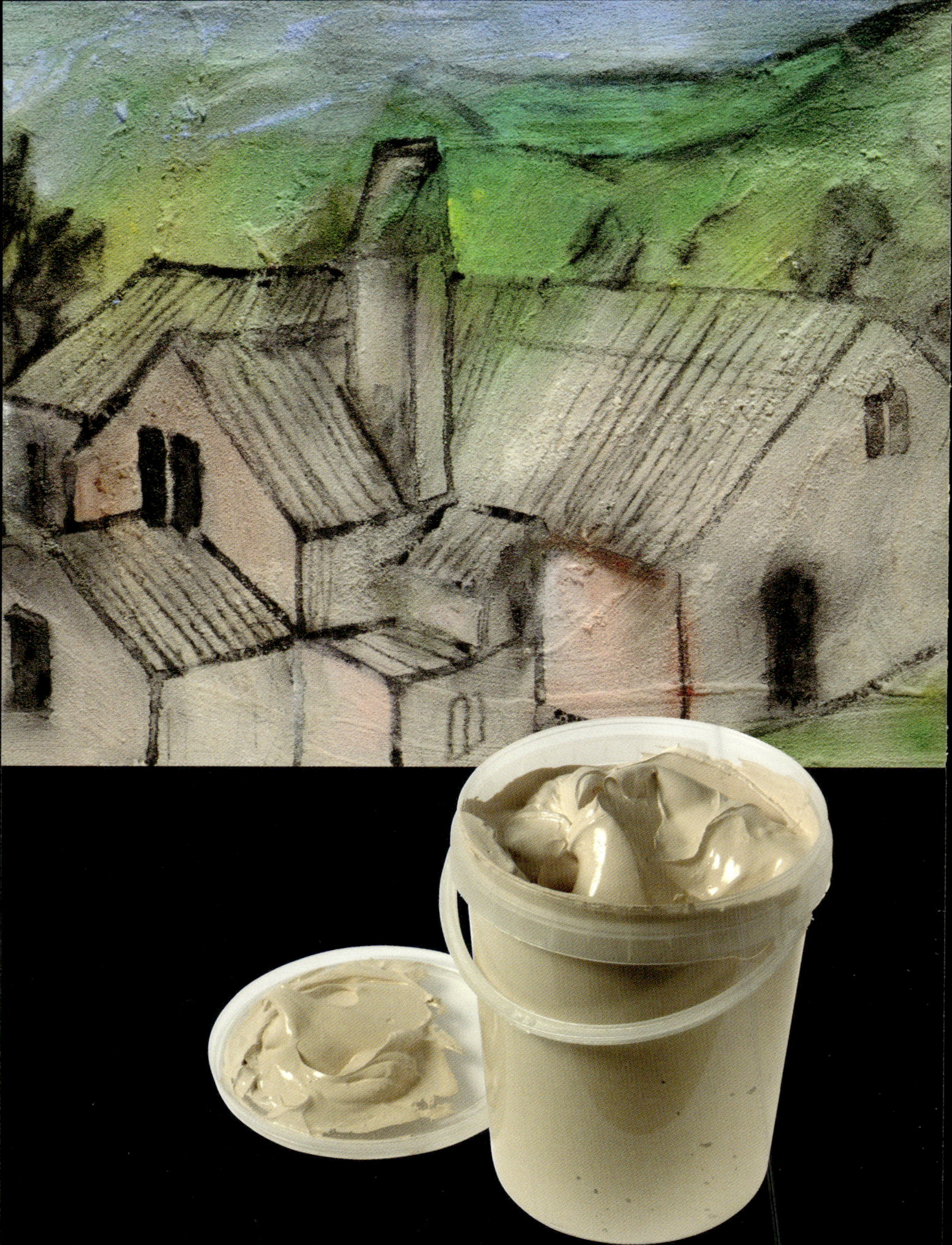

Choosing the Support

The support plays a fundamental role when it comes to texture. Although these days canvas is the most popular support for paintings with texture, rigid boards are generally more permanent and will allow you to incorporate more materials. With proper priming, cardboard, wood panels, and canvas boards provide more permanent bases than flexible fabrics do. If you want the layers of texture to last permanently, the support should be very durable and stable. Consider choosing bases that already have a certain amount of surface relief, since you can take advantage of the actual qualities of the base material. However, since most supports are smooth, we will start here by showing you how to prepare some very interesting textured bases from scratch.

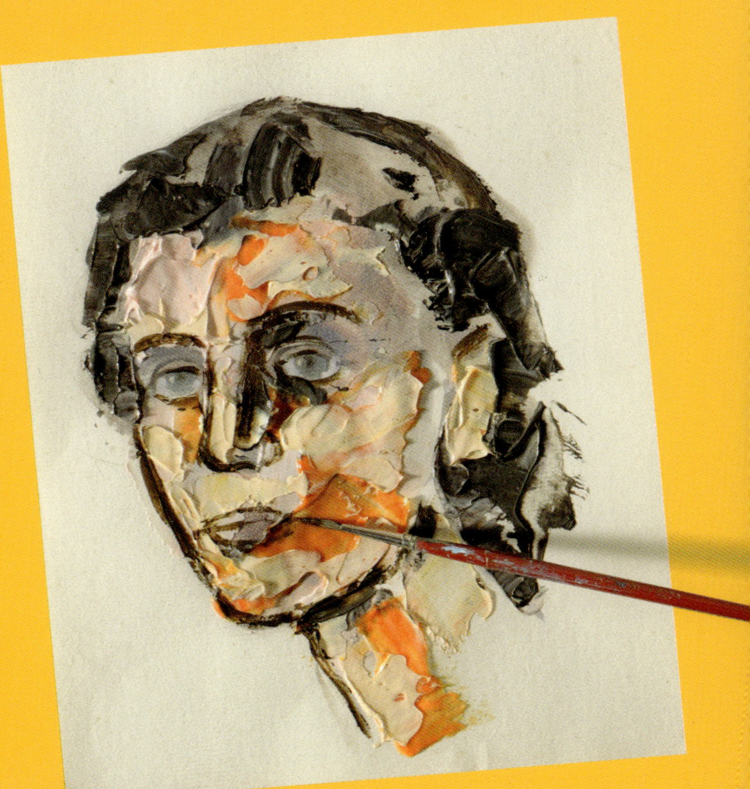

Supports with Relief

Before starting to create a texture, it is important to take some time to choose and prepare the support; the effects that you wish to achieve depend on it. The texture found naturally on many support materials can also be incorporated right into your paintings.

Cardboard does not always have a smooth surface. *Some are corrugated and striated and you can paint over this regular relief.*

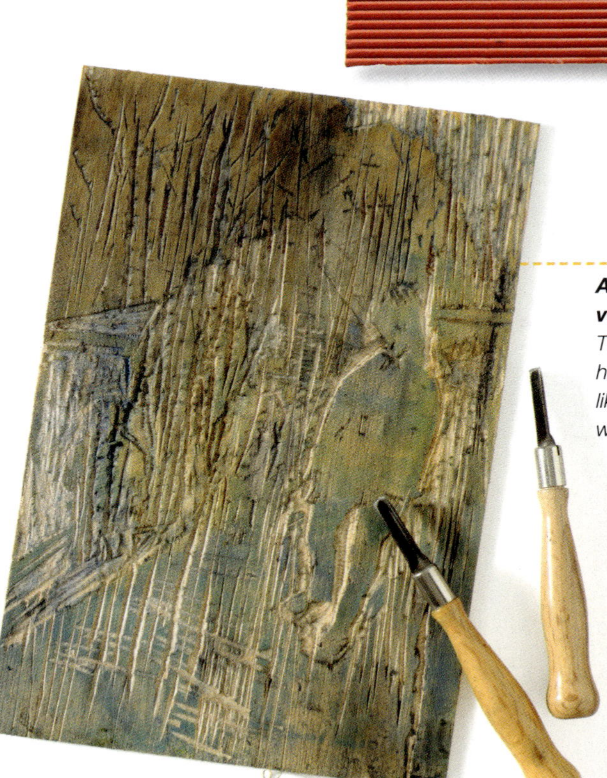

A plywood board can have a very interesting surface grain. *The bas-relief effect can be highlighted by carving with a gauge like those used for making woodcuts.*

The Right Support

It is very important that the support you select be rigid and inflexible; it must not warp and twist, nor fracture and crack, the layered textures. This means avoiding canvas or fabrics that are not tightly stretched on a frame and lightweight papers. Cardboards, heavier papers with rough textures, and boards with pronounced graining are all good options. As a bonus, they have characteristic textures that can be integrated in the artwork.

Textured Supports

Some supports already have a pattern or natural surface relief resulting from their manufacture. In general, it is more complicated to paint on these surfaces, since the relief keeps the paint from covering the entire support uniformly. On the other hand, they offer interesting textures that can be incorporated into the painting in an original way.

Corrugated cardboard offers many possibilities. *If you remove the top layer of paper, the corrugated layer will become visible. This can be cut and glued onto more cardboard to create a textured background. The texture can be softened with a base coat of gesso.*

In this simple model painted in oil *we chose to make use of the relief created by the cardboard support, and adapted the composition to it.*

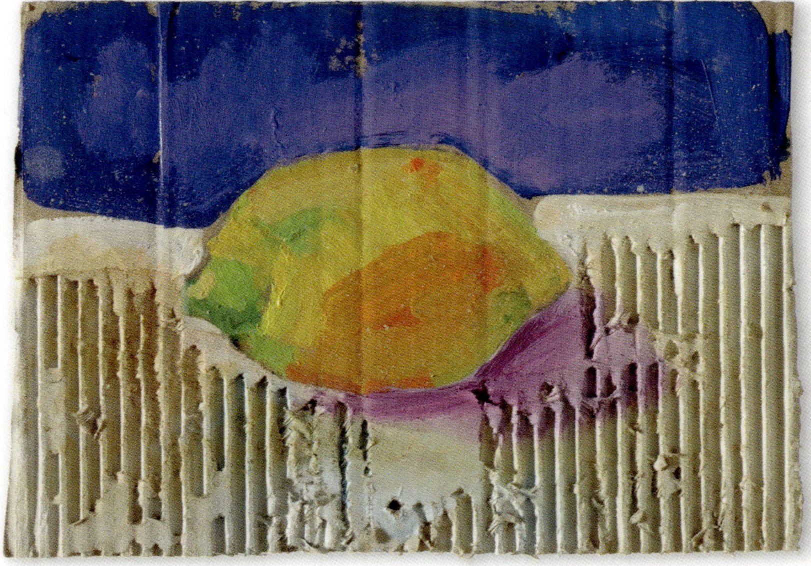

Uniform Texture

Occasionally, a support will possess a strong surface texture that is very interesting. Generally this would consist of a primer with a uniform layer of textured material. Painting on a rough uniform texture is a challenge for any artist, although it often inspires an interest in finding ways to adapt the painting to the characteristics of this surface.

Microspheres are a relatively recent product. *These tiny spheres of glass are mixed with glue or gesso and are used to prime the support while creating a uniformly rough surface.*

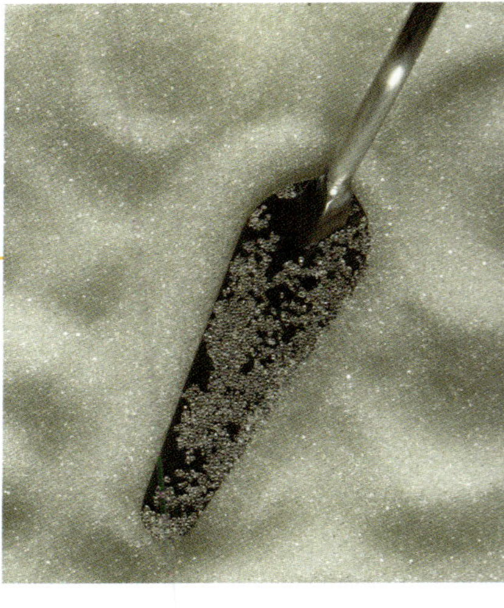

There are other more traditional materials *that, when mixed with latex or white glue, also will make a textured base. The amount of texture created depends on which one you choose to use. From left to right: fine quartz sand, carborundum, and sawdust.*

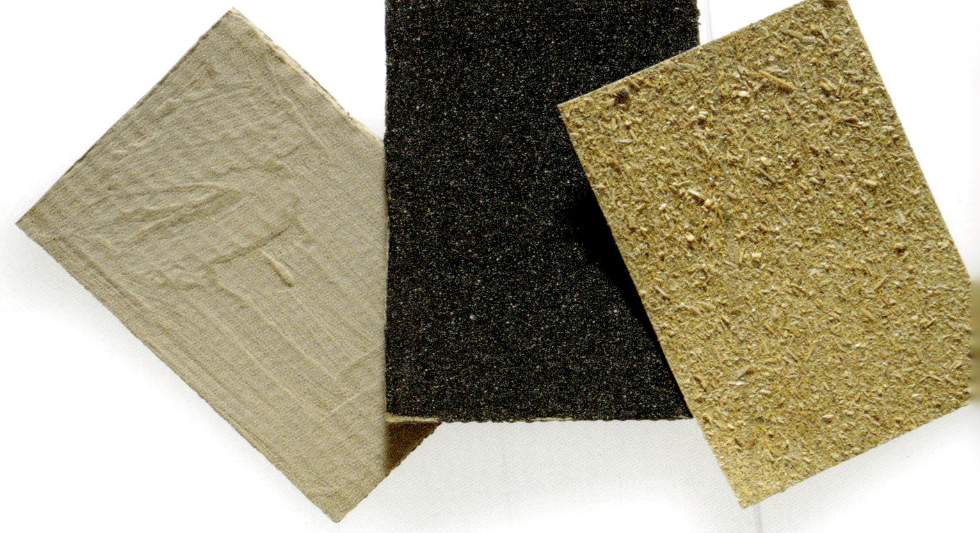

Grainy Backgrounds

A uniformly textured background can be created by mixing well-washed sand (marble dust or fine-grain quartz sand) with gesso or latex glue, and then applying it to the board. Then it can be spread evenly over any surface. A more recently developed product can be found in art supply stores: glass microspheres. They are applied to the support by mixing them with glue, gesso, or paint to form miniscule, spherical, transparent nodules on the painting.

Backgrounds with Lines

There are other ways to texture a support before using it. For example, one typical method is to spread quite a heavy layer of gesso on the surface and mark it with the edge and point of a spatula. The lines should be regular and repeated, so that the entire surface has the same relief effect. You can also use scrapers, combs, or painter's rollers, or make marks with a plastic spatula in any shape you wish in the still-wet primer coat.

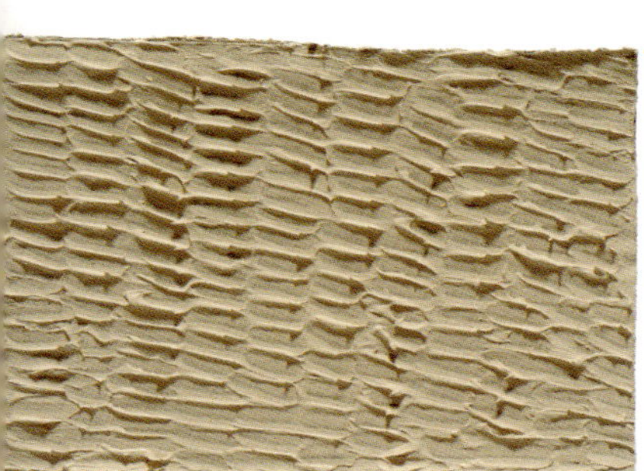

***On a wet gesso background** the rounded point of a spatula is tapped to create a surface with a repetitive and uniform texture.*

***Covering the support with a fine fabric** like gauze or tarlatan will create a fairly uniform threadlike grid. The relief is very subtle, making it very pleasant to paint on it.*

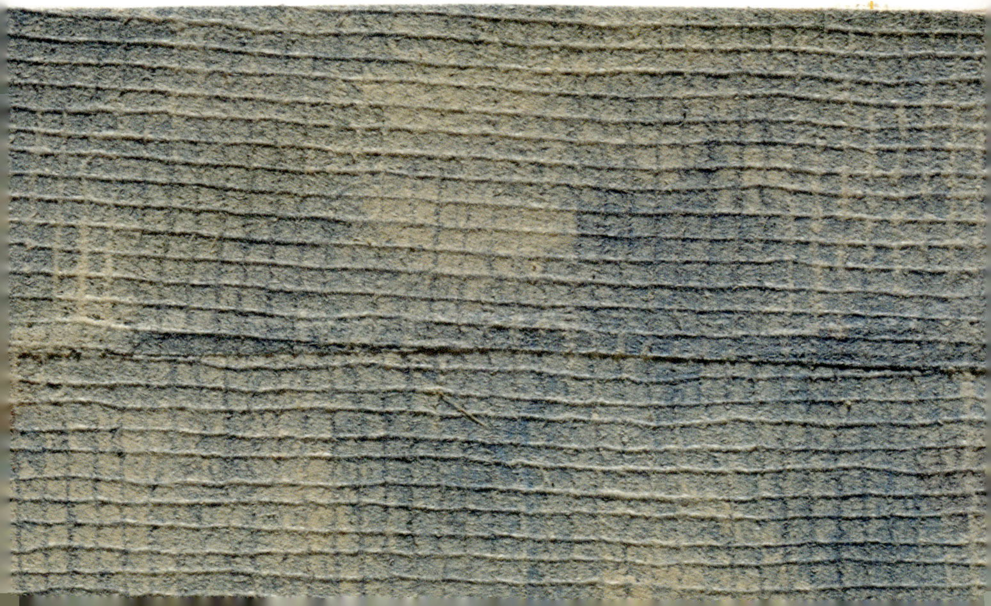

Building Up the Surface Texture

So far, you have seen how to obtain a few basic textures that can be used to prepare the support before starting to paint. In the following section you will learn how to highlight and emphasize these textures with the first layers of paint, highlighting even more, if appropriate, the effect suggested by the relief in the primer coat.

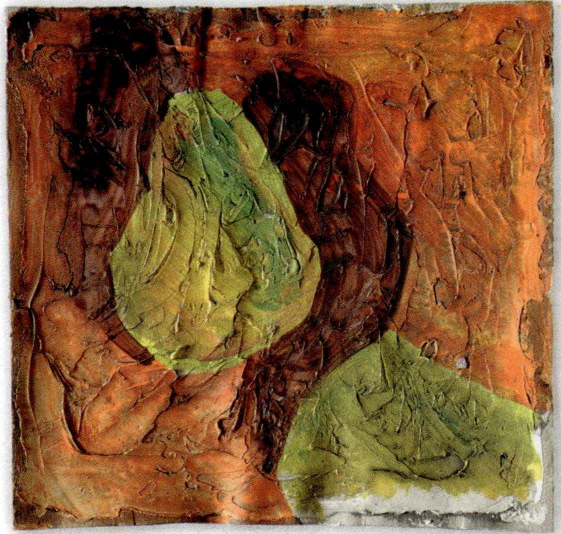

A patina of oil paint diluted in turpentine on a rugged surface of gesso or modeling paste will highlight the relief. *The diluted paint tends to accumulate in the low areas, emphasizing the high areas on the support even more.*

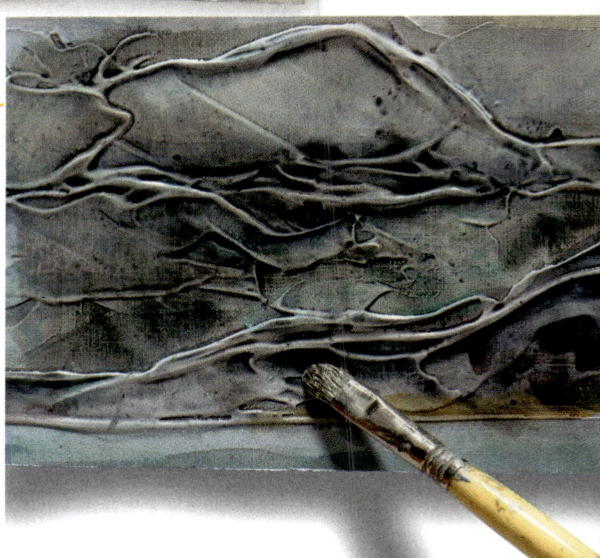

To highlight the relief with diluted paint, *the surface on which you are working should be completely dry and white in color, since the layers of applied color will be very transparent.*

Caught in the Cracks

You can emphasize any texture made with a layer of gesso or modeling paste after it has completely dried. All you have to do is dilute acrylic paint with water, or oil paint with turpentine, and apply a fine layer of color over the whitish surface of the material. The watery paint will flow down and become deposited or trapped among the cracks and incisions in the gesso. Tinting a relief surface with diluted paint is also very effective when the area is covered with wrinkled paper. The differences in color and the contrasts highlight and strengthen the effect of the wrinkles.

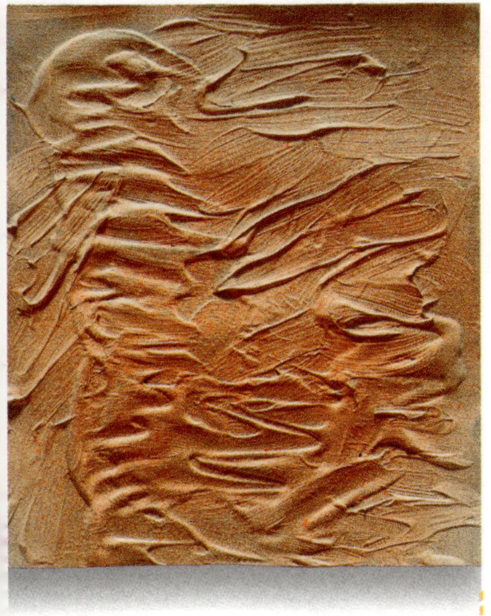

To increase the feeling of relief on a surface *you can spray paint from a can at a low angle. This way the paint will adhere to only one side of the raised texture.*

Spray Paint on Textured Backgrounds

There is another approach to highlighting the bas-relief on the surface of the gesso or modeling paste. Spraying paint perpendicularly on a rough background will emphasize its texture even more. Try spraying yellow paint and then red in the same direction on an opaque white textured background. The resulting orange on the high areas will make the texture stand out, even in neutral light.

Spray paint can also be used on a combed background or on corrugated cardboard. *If you spray a white support with orange paint from one side, the result will be an optical combination of the two colors.*

LET'S EXPERIMENT

Washes on a Sand Background

The subject is an interior with a very tight composition. It is simple and has interesting lighting effects.

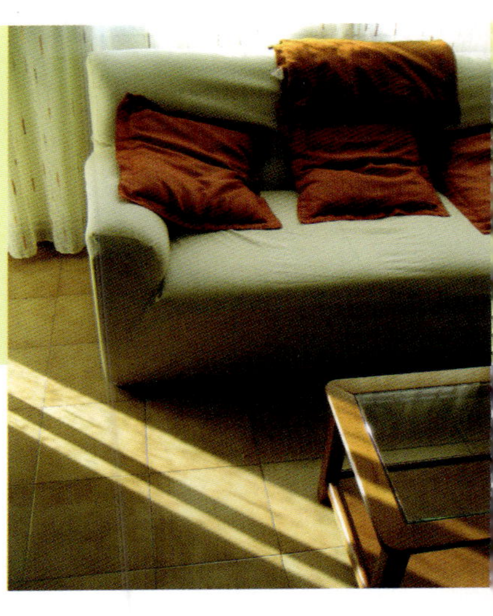

THE CHALLENGE OF TEXTURE

1

1. *To prepare the texture, first cover the support with a creamy layer of white glue. While the surface is still wet, sprinkle on beach sand or finely ground quartz. Let it dry for one hour.*

2

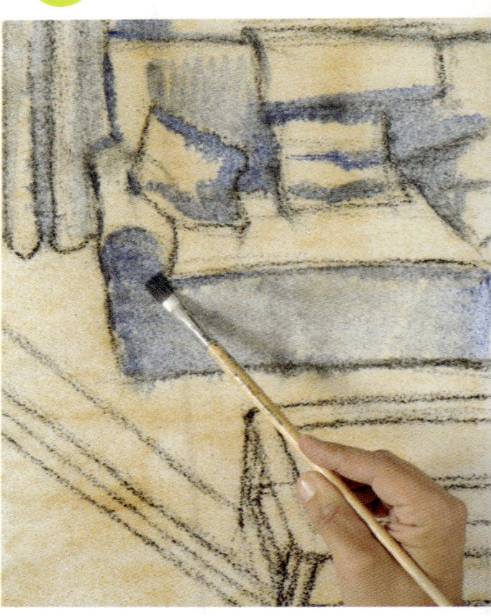

2. *Sketch the main shapes of the model with a stick of charcoal. Then paint the areas in shadow with ultramarine blue that is very diluted with turpentine. You should use a stiff brush since the grainy surface tends to destroy brushes with softer hair.*

A base of latex and fine sand will provide a uniformly grainy background. This is a good way to compare the difference between painting on a prepared texture and painting on a smooth canvas, and observing how the paint acts on each. In this exercise we have chosen an interior without too many elements. Since we are working on an unfamiliar type of surface, it is best to work with a relatively simple model.

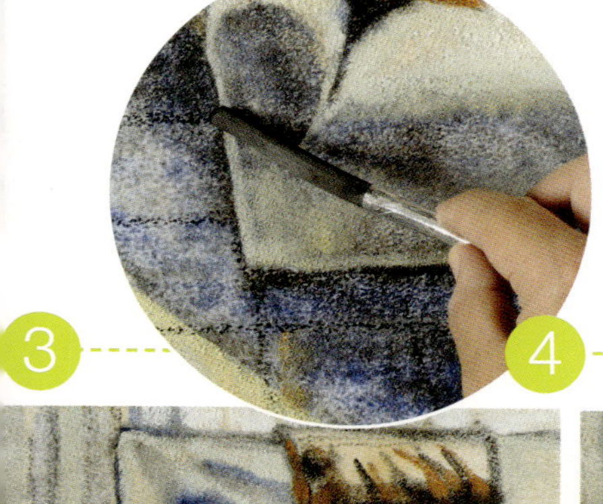

4. *The sofa is finished with light blue tones, paying close attention to the volume and the wrinkles of the cushions, as well as to the different tones of brown on the table. A charcoal stick is used to draw a grid on the floor.*

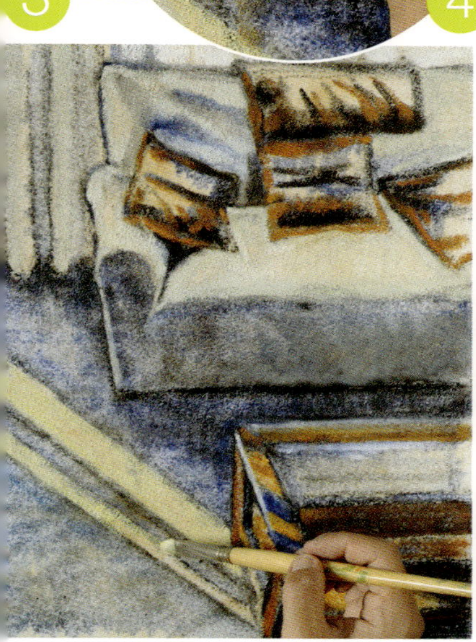

3. *The brown colors are added to the furniture and cushions. Light ocher is used to paint the streaks of sunlight on the floor. The work should be quite stylized, building up the strokes of paint. The sandy surface does not allow for much detail.*

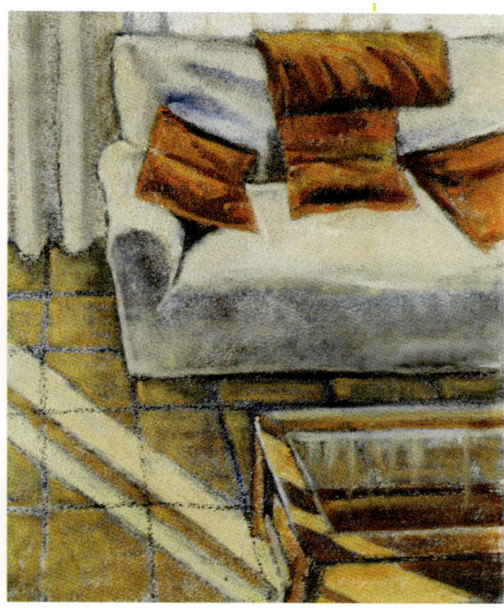

5. *Gabriel Martín uses a finer brush to add the final touches. Very light gray is used to note the reflections on the glass on the table, and ocher lightened with white is used to paint the squares of the tile floor.*

Fabric or Paper Wrinkles

If you intend to combine collage with painting, you do not have to settle for just a single fabric or paper; you can use several to make different colors and textures. It is a good idea to learn how to properly adhere them to the support and how to create wrinkles that achieve an optimal relief effect.

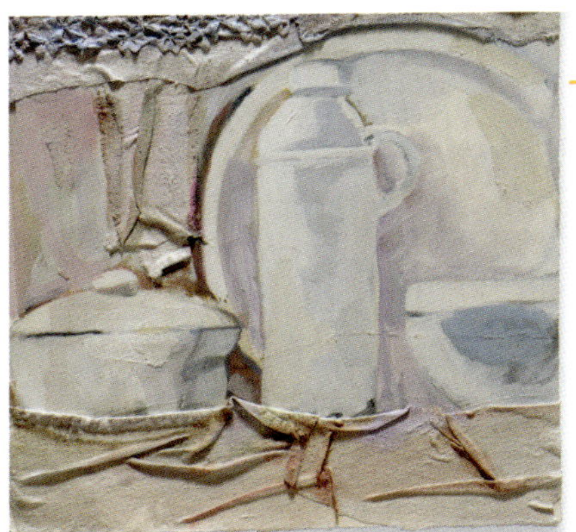

Collage with wrinkled fabric can be incorporated into a still life *to precisely represent the folds and wrinkles of the linen on the table. This is a way of playing with the representation of reality while adding to the attractiveness of the composition.*

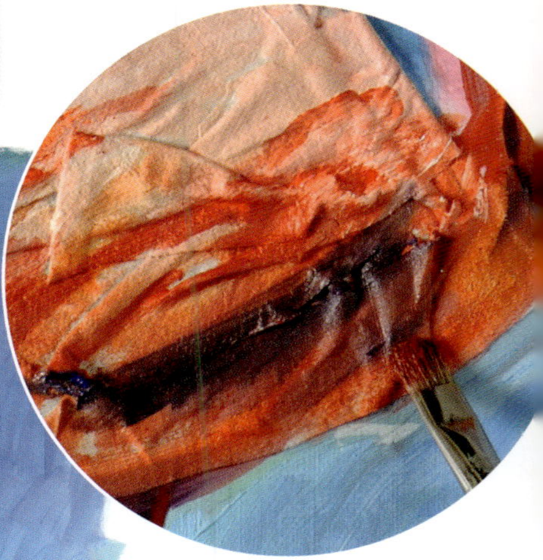

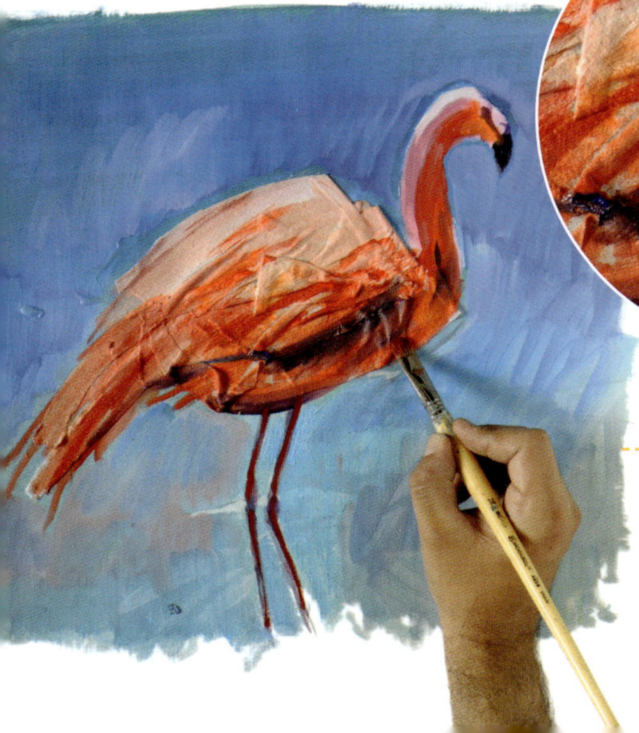

Here we make use of the direction of the fabric folds *to indicate the direction and distribution of the feathers on the flamingo.*

Combing Different Fabrics

Making collages with fabrics of different weaves, weight, and color is a guarantee of texture. They should be glued to the support with acrylic or latex-based glue, or even white glue. Fabrics should be adhered securely underneath and soaked well with diluted glue on top. They can be manipulated while they are still wet to create the wrinkles you need. There is no need to limit yourself to just one fabric—the collage will be more attractive if there are a variety of fabrics. Using fabrics of different qualities and weights will make some wrinkles stiff and geometric and others soft and undulating.

The Role of Silk

Silk has unique abilities for creating transparencies and textures with relief. When it is adhered to any support with water-soluble glue it will contract and wrinkle in very natural ways, forming a relatively uniform blanket of small creases that repeat continuously. Its thinness and light consistency make it very useful for making color transparencies and overlays, much like glazes, with the added effect of a wrinkled texture.

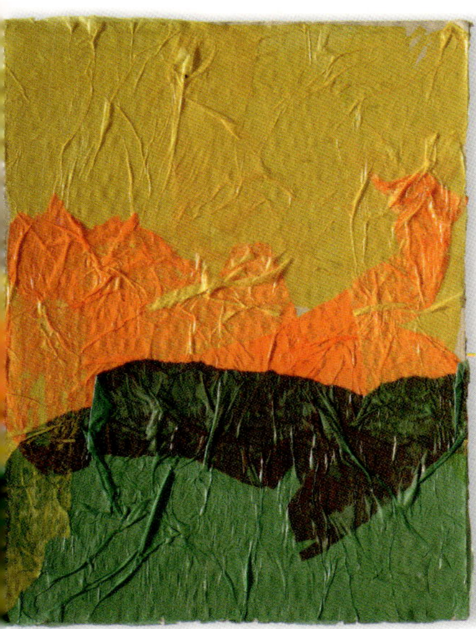

Volume with Wrinkled Paper

Papers with wrinkles and folds can be glued to the surface of the painting with a large amount of latex or white glue. They are generally used to create volume, and often are used as filler for fabrics and tissue paper to increase the amount of relief.

Tissue paper is the most malleable paper for working in collage *and it creates very interesting wrinkles. Since it is very thin and transparent it can also be used for creating glazing effects.*

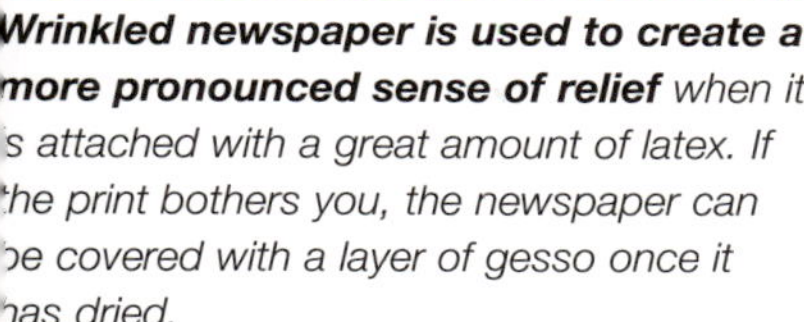

Wrinkled newspaper is used to create a more pronounced sense of relief *when it is attached with a great amount of latex. If the print bothers you, the newspaper can be covered with a layer of gesso once it has dried.*

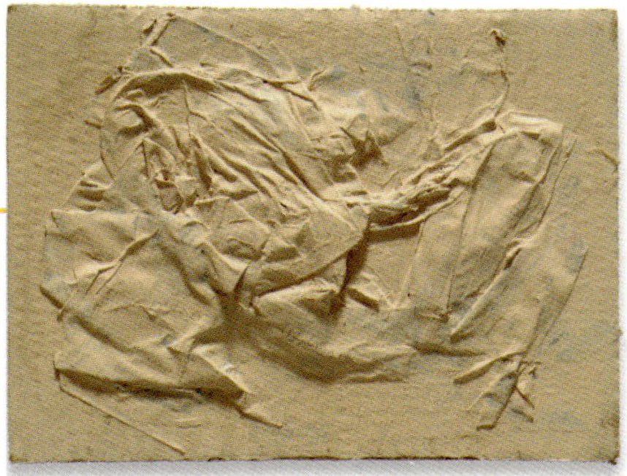

LET'S EXPERIMENT

Painting on Wrinkled Paper

This sunny street juxtaposes colored facades and strong contrasts of light and shadow.

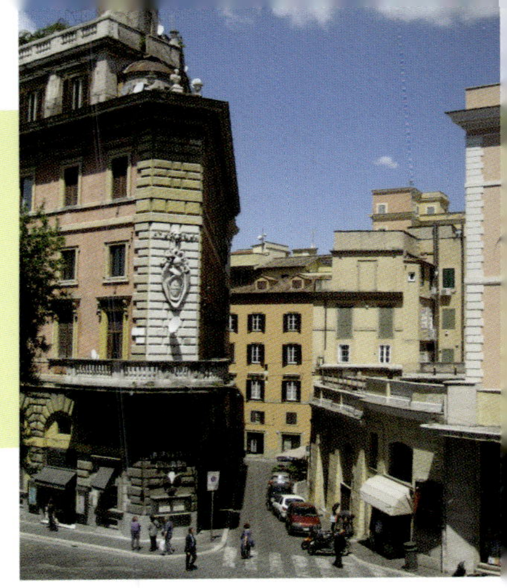

1

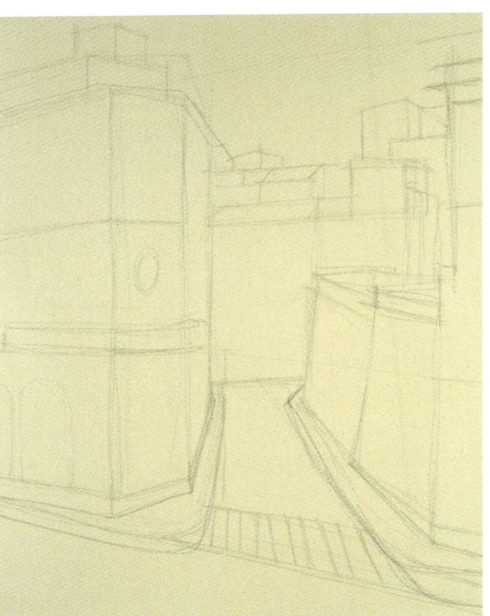

***1.** Draw the architectural forms of the buildings with a pencil. Treat them as simple geometric volumes in perspective. The painting will be very expressionistic, which means that you can take a certain amount of freedom with the drawing.*

2

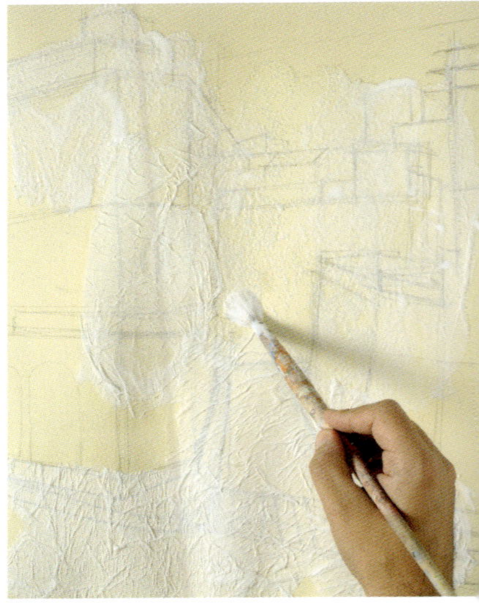

***2.** The pencil drawing will serve as a guide for applying a thin layer of absorbent paper (such as paper towel or toilet paper) that has been soaked with latex glue.*

***3.** Distribute the microspheres in a controlled manner over the wet glue. After a couple of hours, when everything has dried, the paper and the spheres will become more transparent and you will be able to see the preliminary drawing again.*

Now that you are familiar with the different approaches that exist for preparing textured backgrounds, we will look at how we can combine them with microspheres of glass. We will be incorporating collage onto the support. In this exercise by Gabriel Martín, the bas-relief effect caused by the wrinkles and folds of paper soaked in latex are combined with granulated texture.

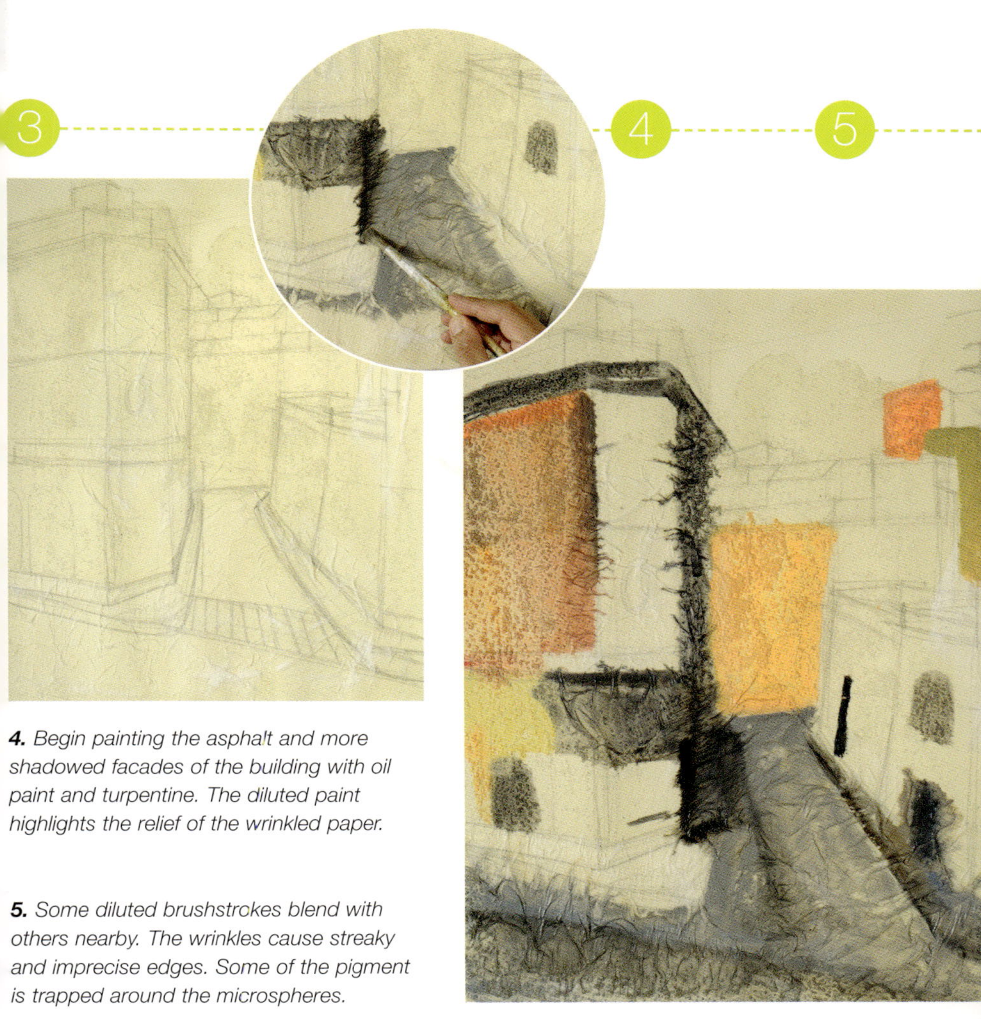

4. Begin painting the asphalt and more shadowed facades of the building with oil paint and turpentine. The diluted paint highlights the relief of the wrinkled paper.

5. Some diluted brushstrokes blend with others nearby. The wrinkles cause streaky and imprecise edges. Some of the pigment is trapped around the microspheres.

LET'S EXPERIMENT

6. Paint the lightest facades with very light ochers, grays, and browns. As the painting progresses, use less turpentine with the colors. The microspheres create an interesting texture on the front of the building on the left.

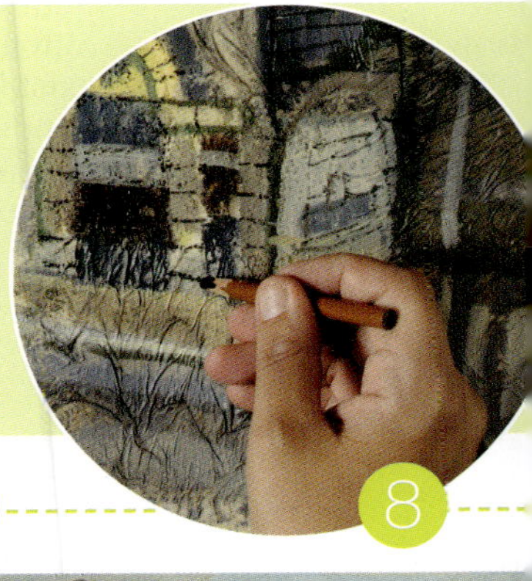

6

7

8

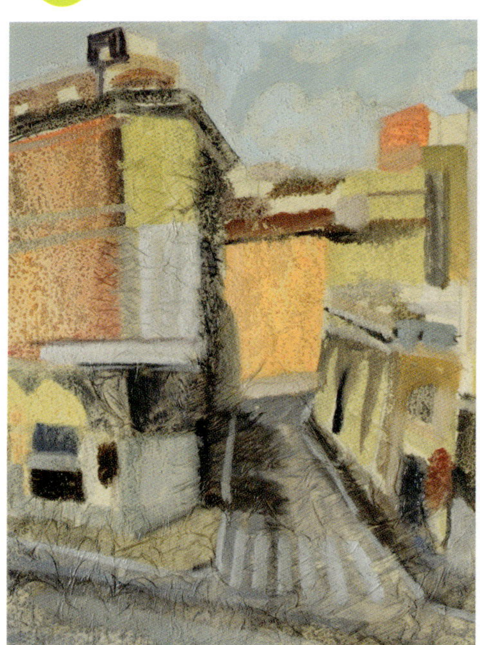

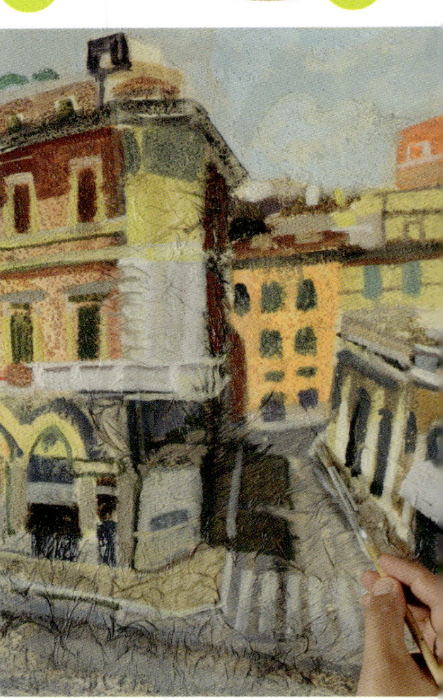

7. Paint the doors, windows, balconies, and some architectural details with a medium round brush. The secret is to base the painting on forms and the contrasting colors, not on the details.

8. *Without waiting for the paint to dry, draw some lines to better define the architecture of the buildings with a Conté oil base pencil. These lines should coincide with the lines of perspective.*

9. *Using a fine brush, Gabriel Martín applied some final strokes of pure white, on some window frames, on the railings of the balconies, and on the awnings of the shops. In the finished painting you can see how the texture is the most dynamic element of the painting.*

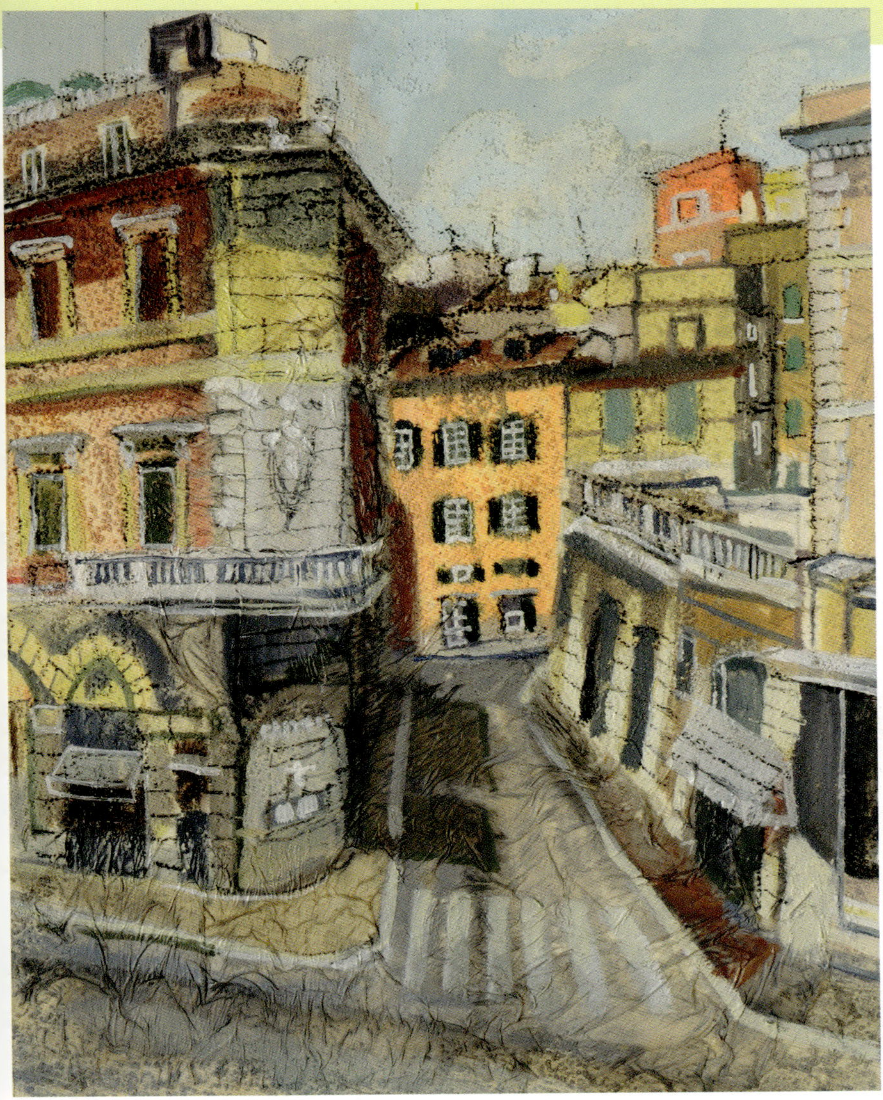

IN THE STYLE OF...

Amadeo de Souza-Cardoso (1887–1918)

Souza-Cardoso was one of the precursors of modern art in Portugal. Although his life was very short, he has always been an influence on the avant-garde painters of his country. Because of family pressure

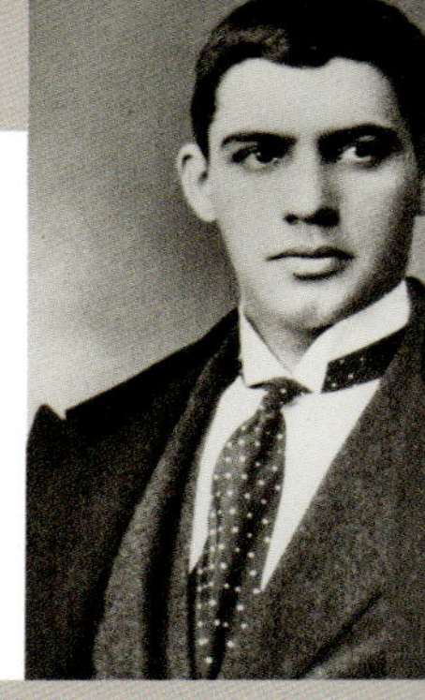

Souza-Cardoso was the main proponent of avant-garde painting in Portugal.

Paris Café *(1908)*
During his stay in Paris, the artist made many sketches, this interior among them. In all of them can be seen great freedom of execution, an attempt to depict the figures with heavy brushstrokes of oil paint. Each person, each part of the body, every corner of the painting is created with a single striated brushstroke, so the surface of the painting has a light relief of furrows created by "combing" with the brush. The light and shadows that reside in the strokes become another component of the painting, altering and enriching the shades of the colors.

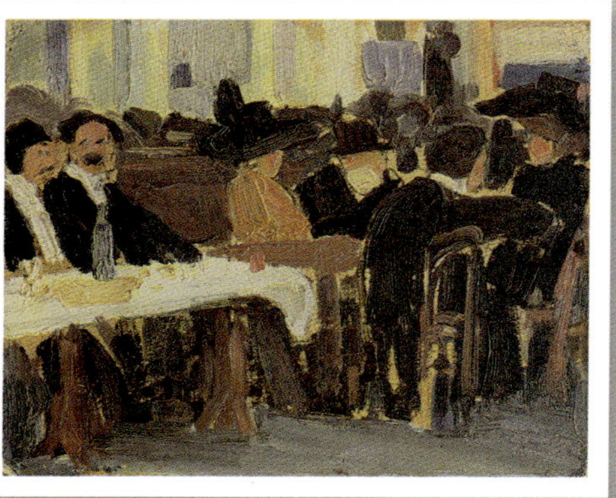

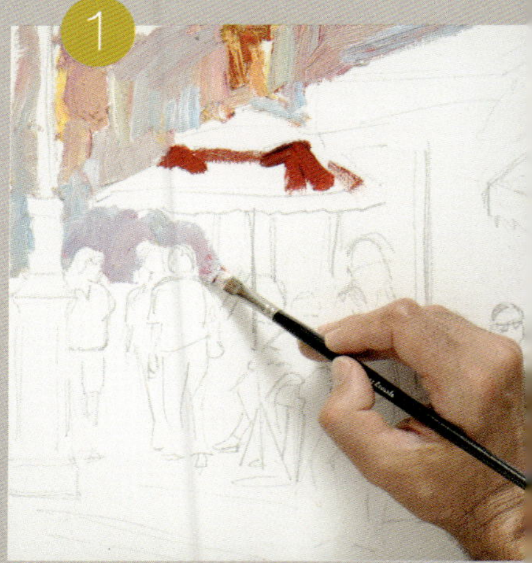

1. *Using brushstrokes similar to those of Souza-Cardoso, paint the terrace of a café with thick oils, so that the marks left by the brush can be seen. When working over a pencil drawing, it is best to begin with the background.*

AN EXPRESSIVITY

he started out studying law, but in 1906 his creative restlessness made him leave everything behind and travel to Paris, where he encountered Impressionism, Expressionism, and Fauvism. In his paintings of Paris cafés, the artist demonstrated a freedom that ignored academic tradition. His expressive works are nearly impastos, with a synthesis of forms created by using masses of thick paint and lively brushstrokes. Despite his exposure to a great many artistic influences, he always managed to demonstrate originality and creativity in his work.

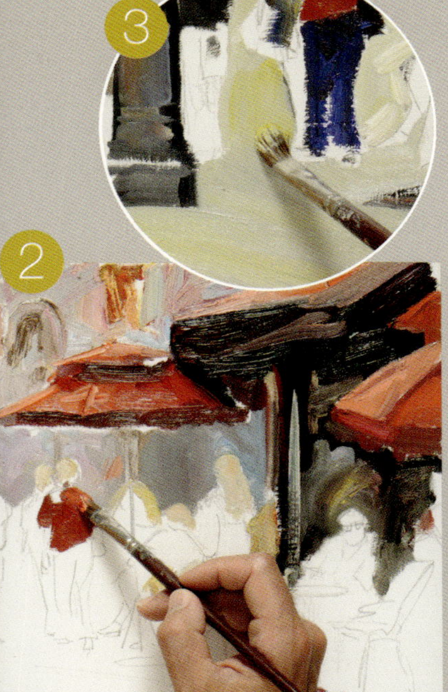

__3.__ The painting should be highly stylized. Each area can be resolved with just a couple of brushstrokes, mixing the colors directly on the support.

__2.__ The brushstrokes should be flatter in the background, but the nearer umbrellas and awnings should be more textured and the brushstrokes more pronounced.

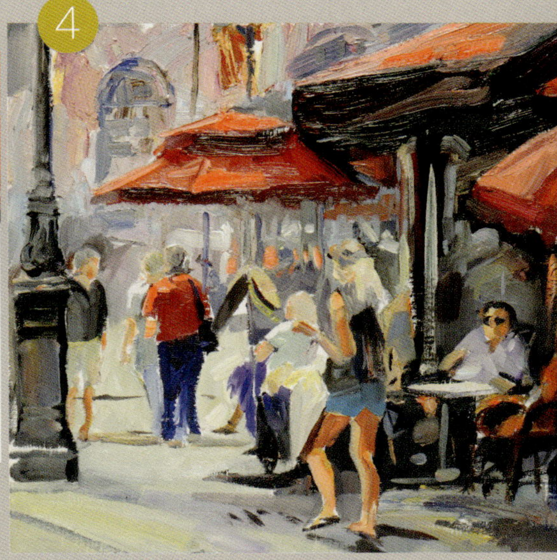

__4.__ You must know when to stop. Do not use too much detail. The thick, lined brushstrokes should be the only protagonists in this representation. This painting was done by Óscar Sanchís.

Backgrounds with Heavy Texture

White glue, latex, mediums, and acrylic paint itself are all strong adhesives, and can be used to easily incorporate many materials into paintings, even those that are larger than sand or microspheres. In this section we will show you some materials, some very surprising, that can be incorporated into the painted surfaces to create heavier textures and greater relief effects.

Carborundum is a material that is sold by the pound in three different grain sizes, *the largest of which can be mixed with latex to create a background covered with a very abrasive granulated texture.*

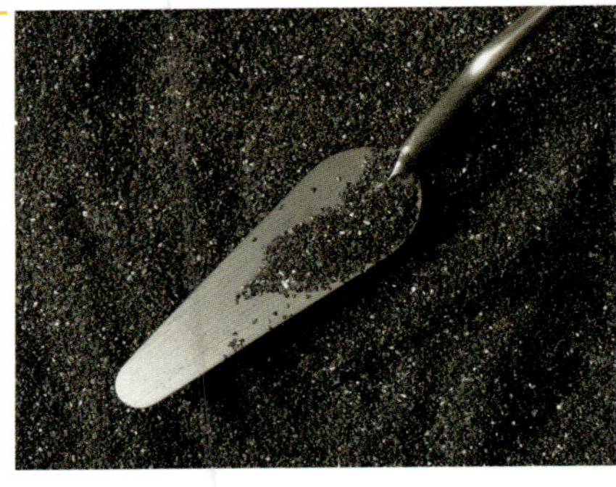

Painting on a surface made using heavy grain marble dust is not easy. *The paint tends to accumulate on the high areas of the texture, and brushes wear out very quickly.*

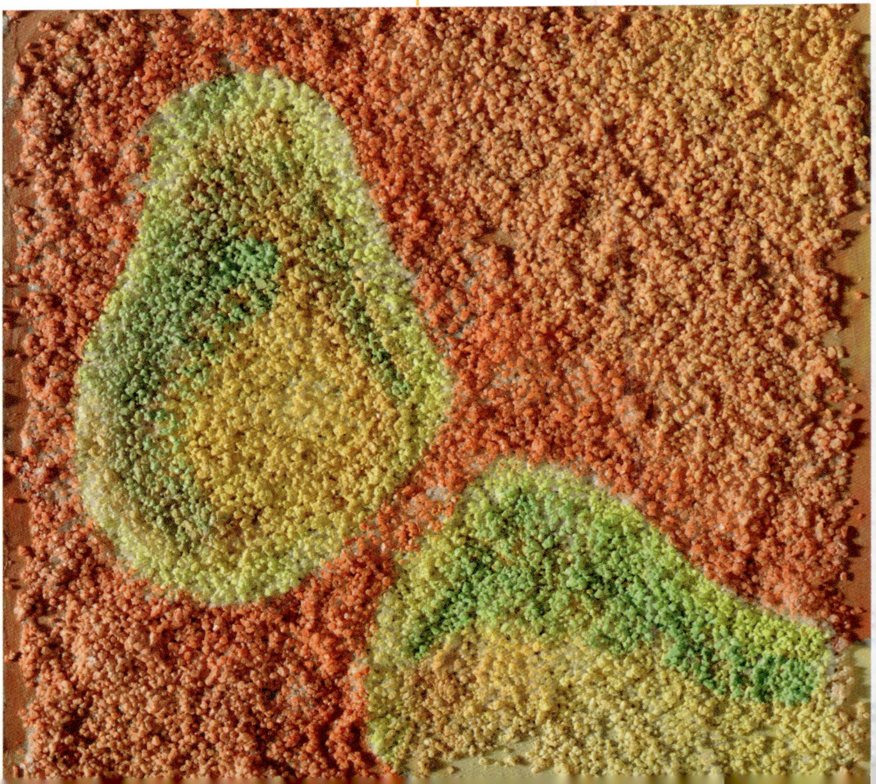

Uncommon Materials

It is common to use heavy grain sand and marble dust; however, there are other less expected materials that can also create a very rich texture. Many of them are more easily found in supermarkets than art supply shops. Among the most interesting are: rice, beans, noodles, small pasta, and sawdust. Working on a surface covered with these bulk materials is not an easy task if you are trying to make a conventional painting. However, they are ideal for artists who wish to create something truly original and striking.

Application Methods

When adding fillers that are very large or heavy you cannot use gesso; it does not have enough adhesive strength and it will crack. It is better to work with thick latex that is undiluted. First you must cover the surface with a large amount of latex and then create texture by incorporating the chosen filler into it. Allow it to dry for several hours, but it still will not be ready for painting. Next you cover it with a new layer of latex to keep any granules from coming off while it is being painted. This new layer will also help by filling the deepest crevices. Here gesso can be used as a sealer instead of latex.

Many unique, uncommon materials *can be used for preparing textured backgrounds. You should experiment with them until you find the most interesting surfaces.*

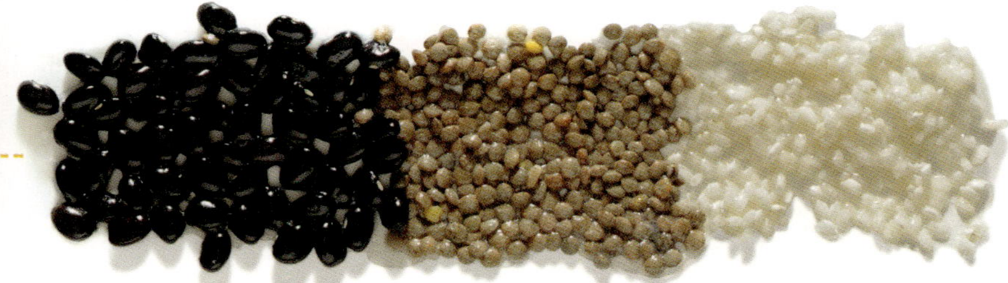

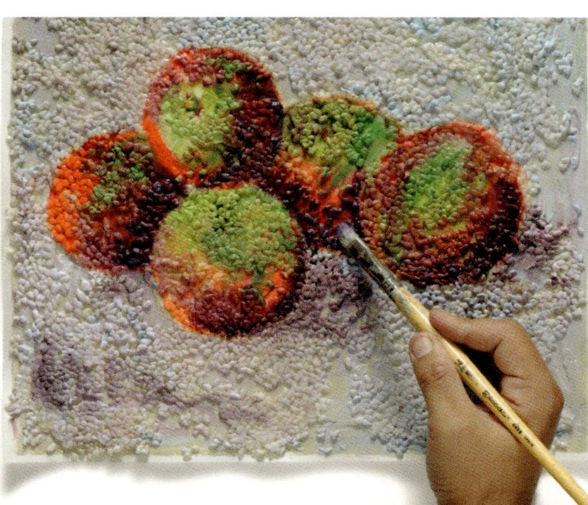

This simple still life was painted on a surface created with rice and latex. *A thick layer of latex was applied to the entire surface to reduce the abrasion and wear and tear on the paintbrushes. Painting over this with oil paint is not very different than painting on a standard support.*

A World of Possibilities

Now that we have looked at the different varieties of textures, we can analyze some of them, studying the ingredients that are used and the way that they interact with the paint. As you will see, there are many possible mixtures of gels, glues, and fillers, and there are many qualities of mediums and gels. However, in this section we will only analyze the varieties of textures and ingredients that can be incorporated into a painting. Here the end justifies the means, since an attractive texture can be made from nearly any mixture of elements, no matter how different they are from each other. The textures shown here were applied with a metal spatula.

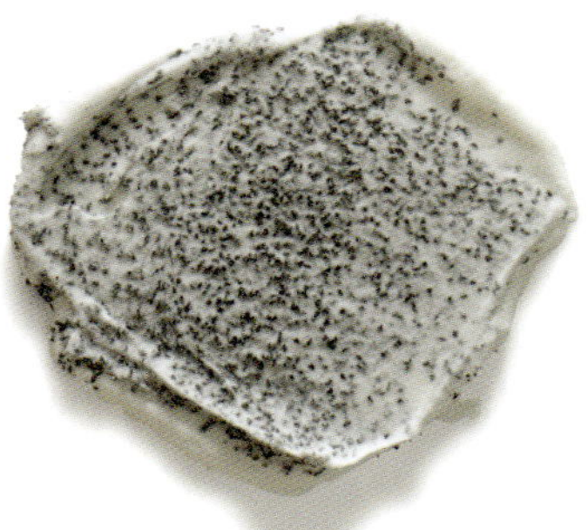

Light modeling paste mixed with carborundum. *This creates a light but abrasive graininess.*

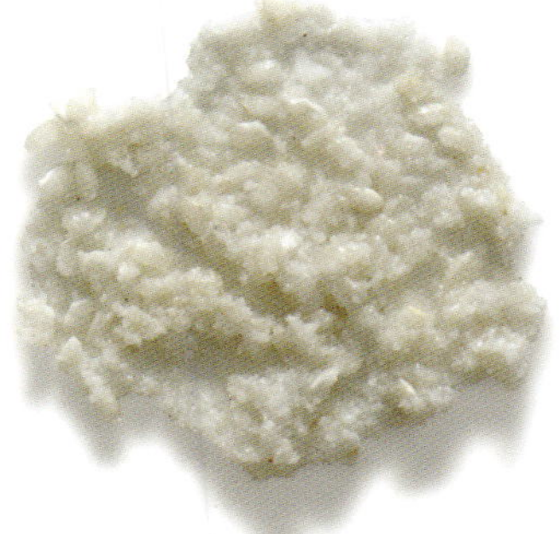

Gel, heavy grain marble dust, and grains of rice. *Mixing two different fillers will create a surface with grains of different sizes.*

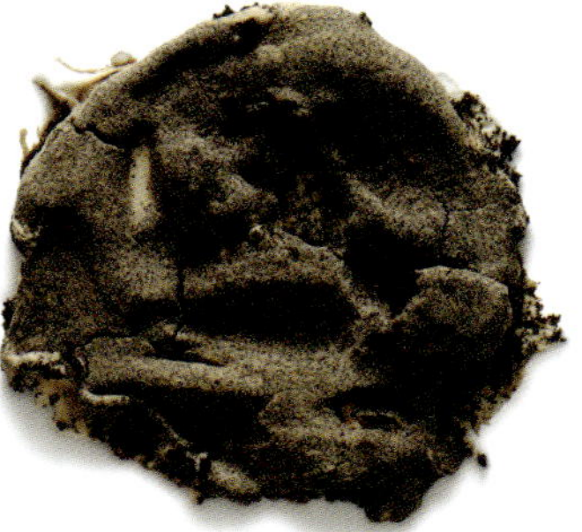

Light modeling paste and coffee grounds. *The filler is used coffee grounds. Although they tend to tint the paste, after it dries they will not mix with the paint colors.*

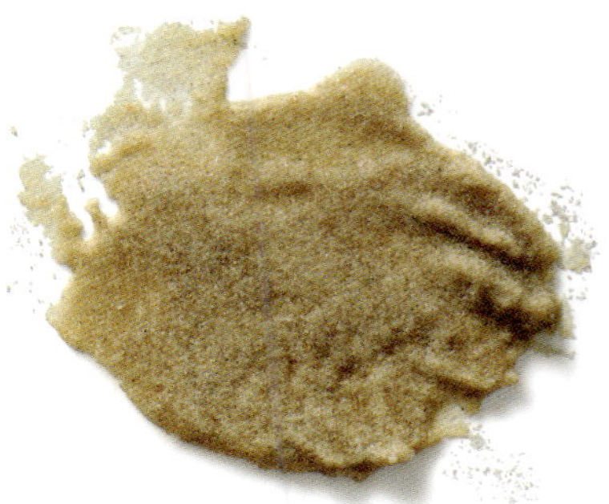

Varnish and fine sand. *Varnish can also be used as a glue or agglutinate. After drying it becomes very hard and is not very flexible.*

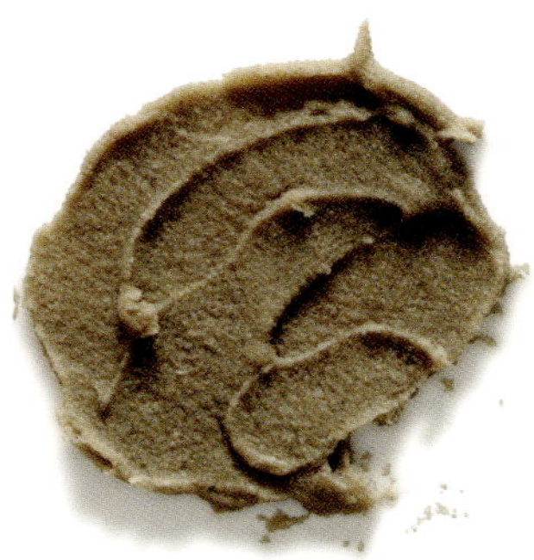

Latex and marble dust. *When dry this mixture has a characteristic gray color and it is very flexible. This texture works very well on fabrics.*

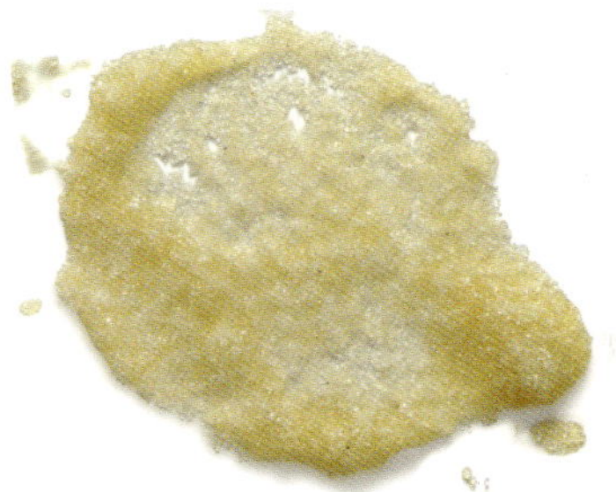

Varnish and microspheres. *Varnish mixed with glass microspheres creates a very transparent finish. The texture is very rigid, but the grain is finer and does not damage paintbrushes.*

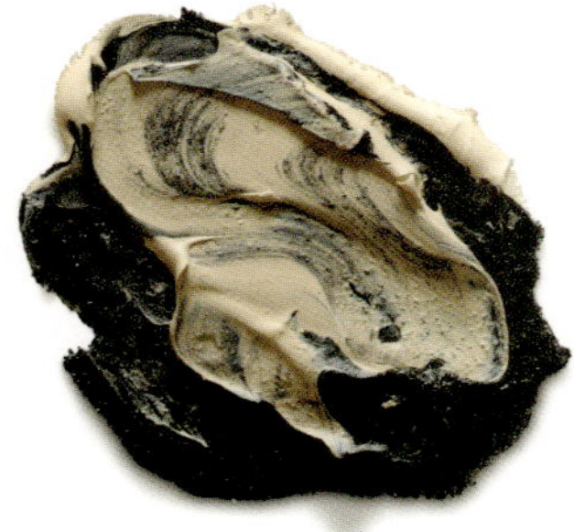

Black lava and gesso. *This deeply black lava has a very fine grain that can be used for working with opaque paint, but it is not recommended for painting with glazes.*

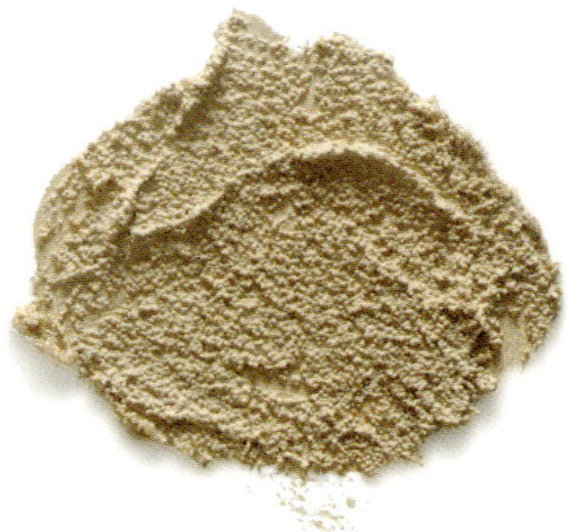

Pink gesso and microspheres. *The gesso has a very light color and highlights the relief of the microspheres. It is ideal for painting with glazes.*

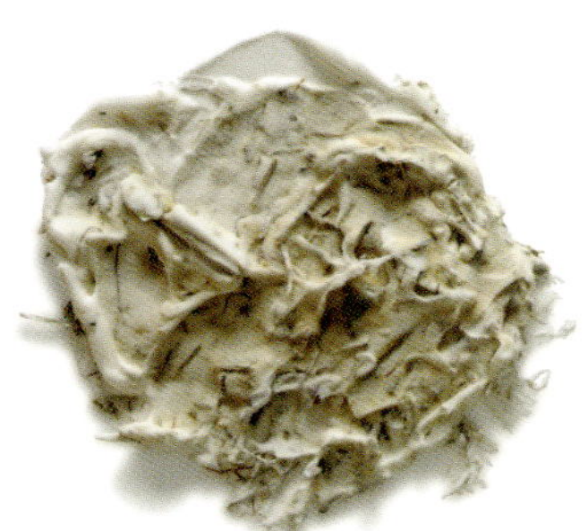

Organic material and light modeling paste. *Finely chopped grass or straw can be incorporated into the mixture, preferably when dry so that the material in the painting will not decompose.*

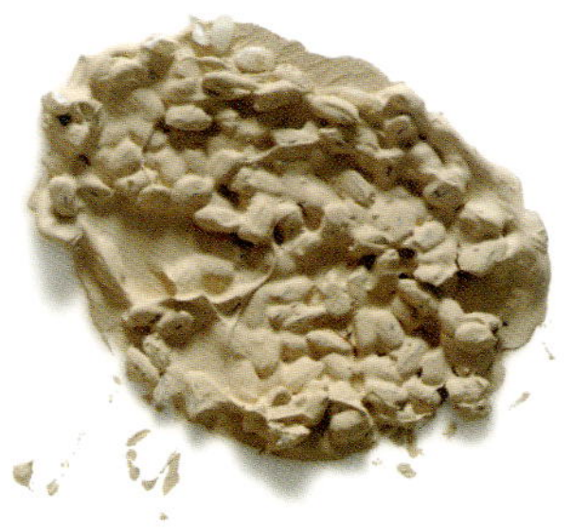

Pink gesso with rice. *Since the gesso has a thick consistency it transposes the grains of rice and makes them look like small nodules or stones. The brush will slide easily across this surface.*

LET'S EXPERIMENT

Still Life with a Textured Gesso Background

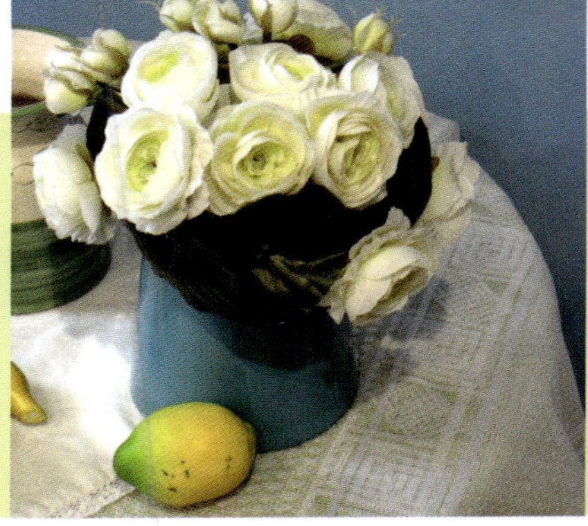

Select a simple model, otherwise the added texture could make the finished product seem too busy.

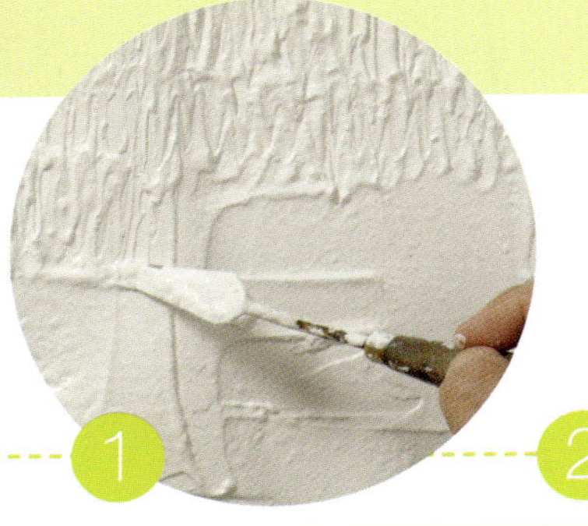

1

2

3

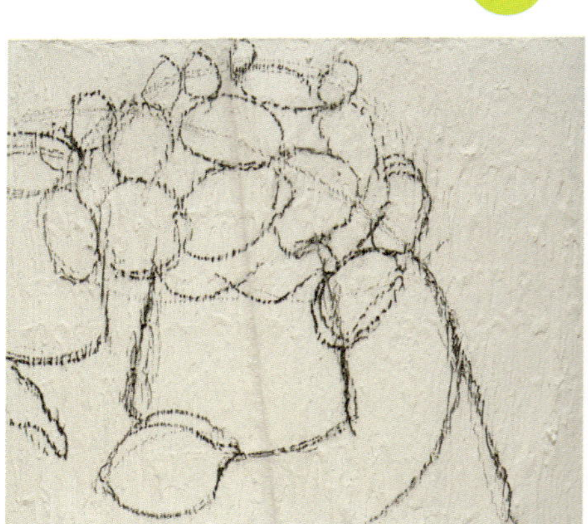

***1.** Cover the entire canvas with quite a heavy layer of gesso. Use the tip of a spatula to create a series of closely spaced lines.*

***2.** Continue to cover the whole surface with the same sgraffito effect to create a uniformly textured surface. Then allow it to dry for a day.*

***3.** Draw a sketch of the model with a charcoal stick on the dry gesso, focusing on the rough shapes and avoiding any details.*

Modeling paste or gesso allows you to prepare a support with a uniformly rough texture. All you need to do is spread on a thick layer and then make repeated marks in it with the rounded tip of a spatula. After the paste completely hardens, it is ready for painting. This effect will make any subject more attractive, especially simple compositions like still lifes. Here Gabriel Martín creates an oil painting exercise with a textured gesso background, and shows the best way to carry it out.

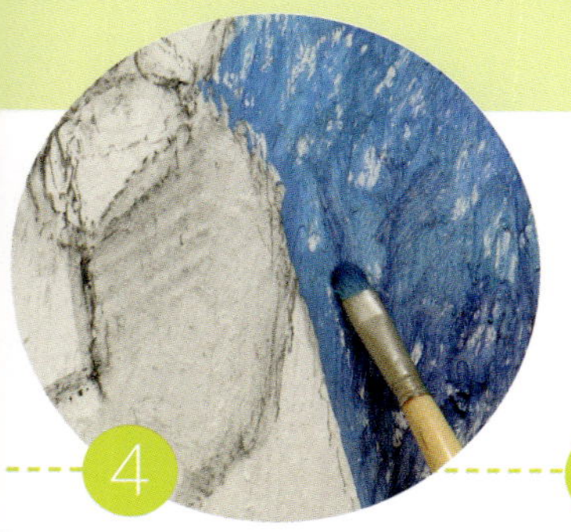

4 5 6

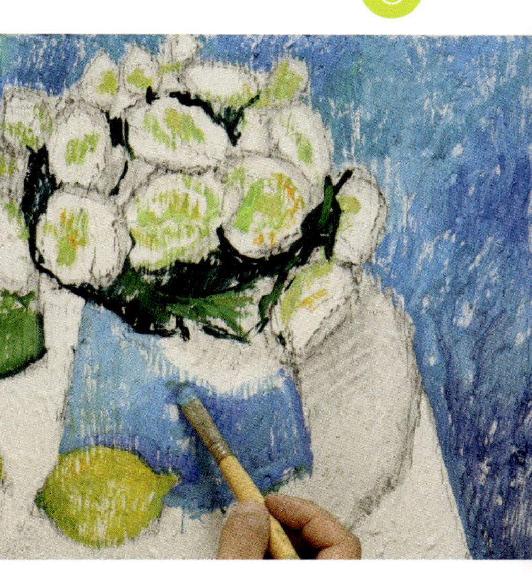

4. Wipe a clean rag over the charcoal to remove the black dust and keep it from muddying the colors. Paint the background with cyan blue and ultramarine blue. The paint should be somewhat diluted with turpentine, but not excessively so.

5. Add the first brushstrokes to the lemon and the flowers using variations of yellow, ocher, and green. Notice how the paint does not completely cover the textured gesso surface. This is precisely the effect you want to achieve.

6. The textured base causes the paint to accumulate on the high areas and leave areas of bare white in the cavities. This impedes a uniform distribution of color and adds a grainy look to the surface of the painting.

7. *While the vase and the background are flooded with blue tones, the shadows take on a more violet coloring. You want each element to stand out because of its saturated and intense color.*

8. *The flowers should not be painted with just white; you should add short strokes of ocher, violet, pink, and yellow, all mixed with a large amount of white.*

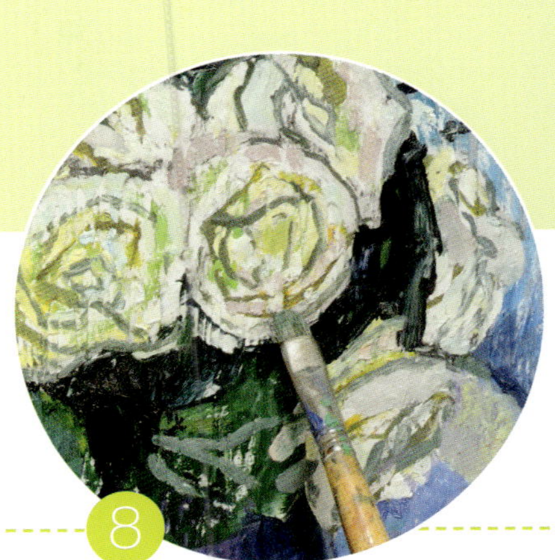

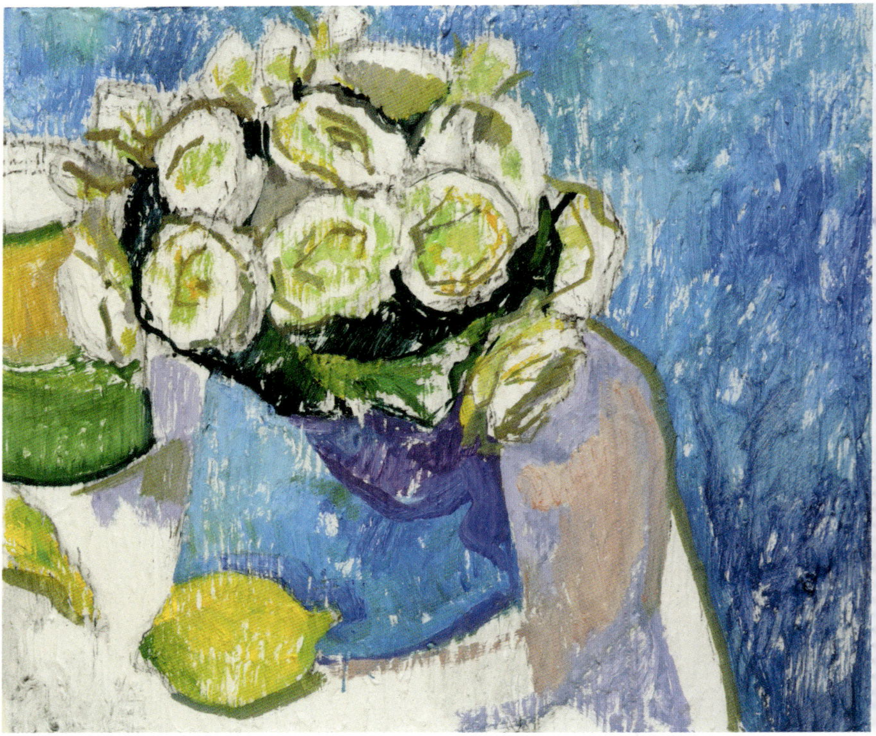

__9.__ What makes this painting special is the black outline added to some elements. The resulting effect is reminiscent of stained glass windows.

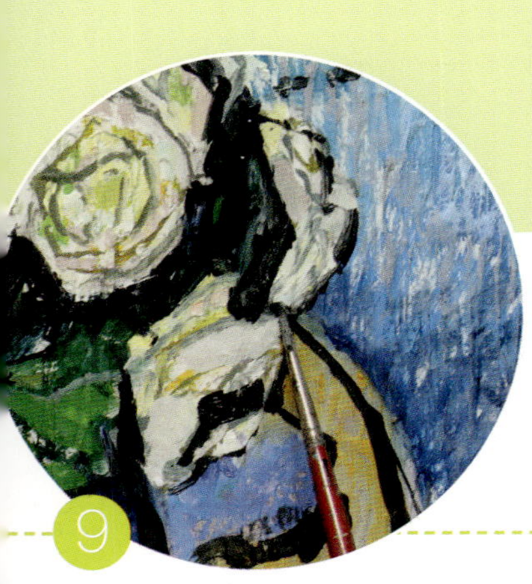

__10.__ The completed oil painting combines the interesting way that color is broken up by the texture of the support with the graphic black brushstrokes dramatically highlightling come of the forms.

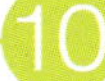

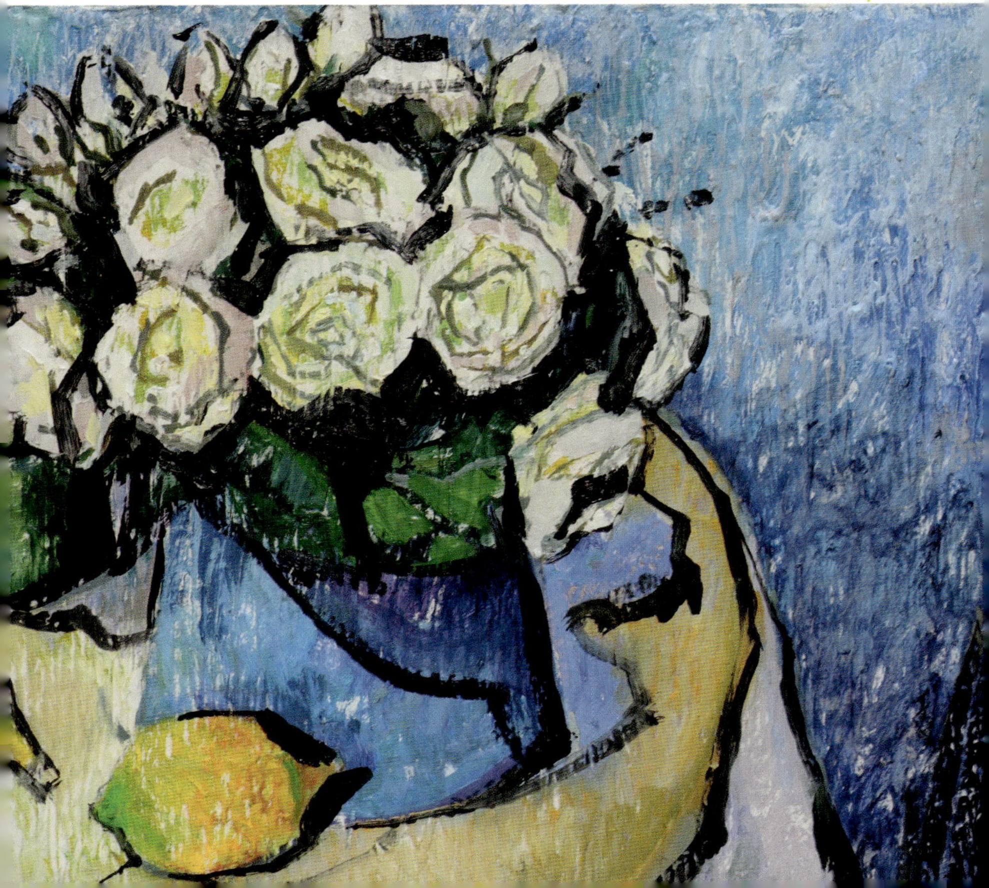

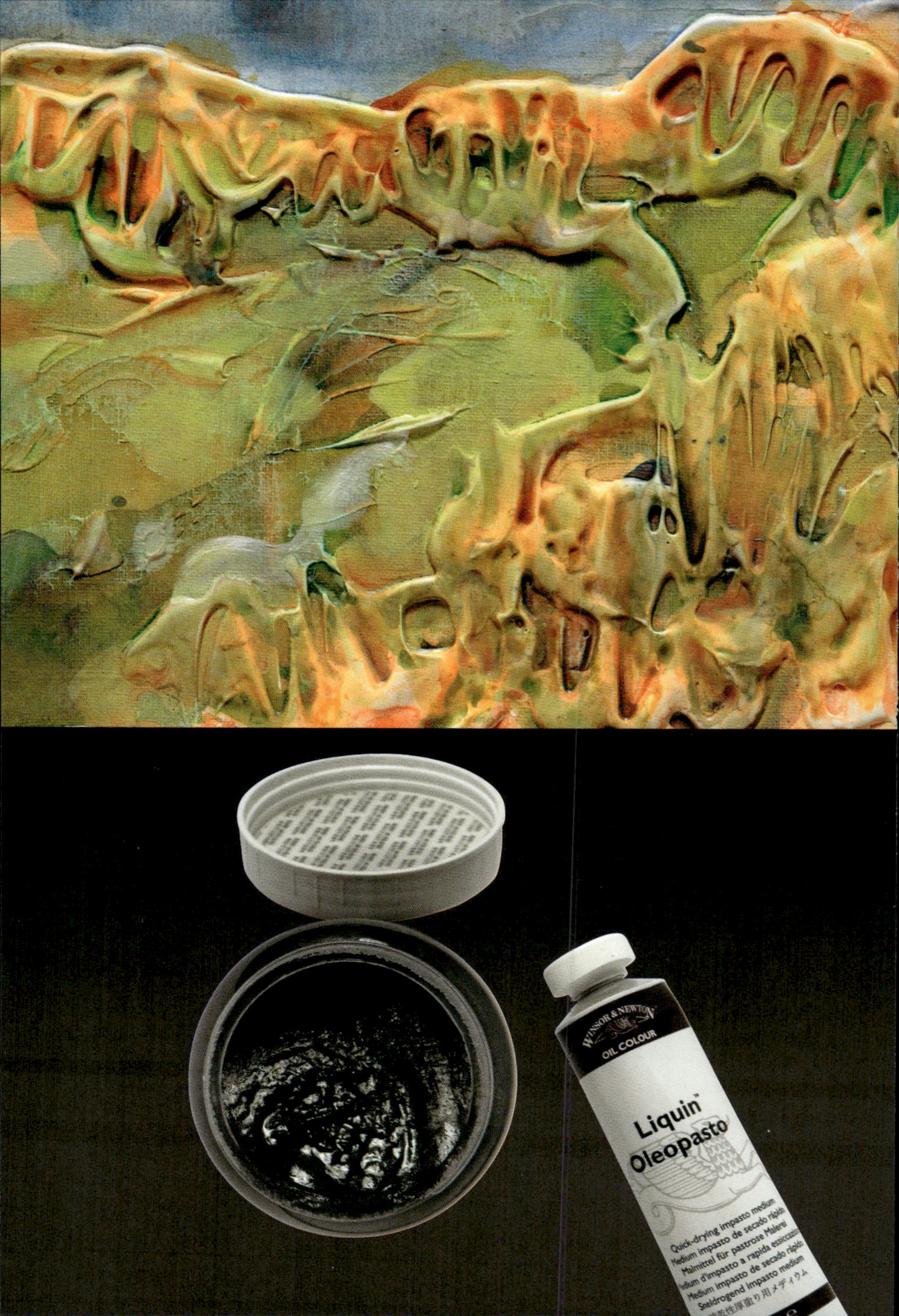
WINSOR & NEWTON
OIL COLOUR
Liquin™
Oleopasto
Quick-drying impasto medium
Medium impasto de secado rápido
Malmittel für pastrose Malerei
Medium impasto de secado rápido
Sneldrogend impasto medium

How to Add Volume to a Painting

It is very difficult to create strong relief on the surface of a painting using only paint itself without wasting a great amount of it, and consequently wasting a lot of money. Although paint is expensive, many substances that can be mixed with it to give it greater volume and alter its consistency are not. These substances are known as mediums and they can increase the range of textures that are made with acrylic and oil paints. In the following chapters we present a complete selection of these modifiers of fluidity and volume that are used to add relief paintings.

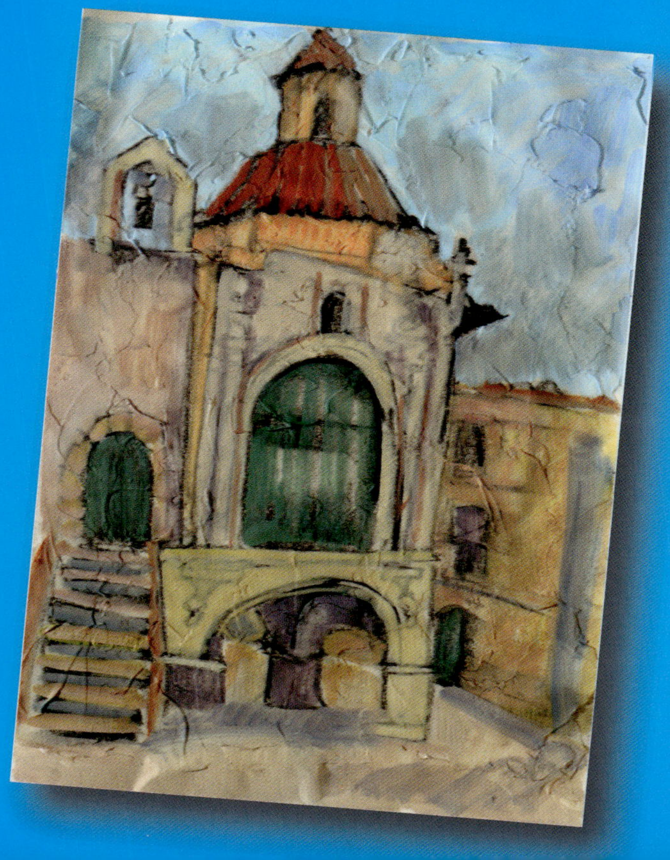

Mediums and Gels: Modifiers of Fluidity

These thick creamy substances are added to acrylics and oils to give them different consistencies and to add volume to the finishes. They are sold in different viscosities and in gloss, satin, and matte finishes. Many mediums are versions of the same emulsion, making them quite safe to mix with paints or with each other.

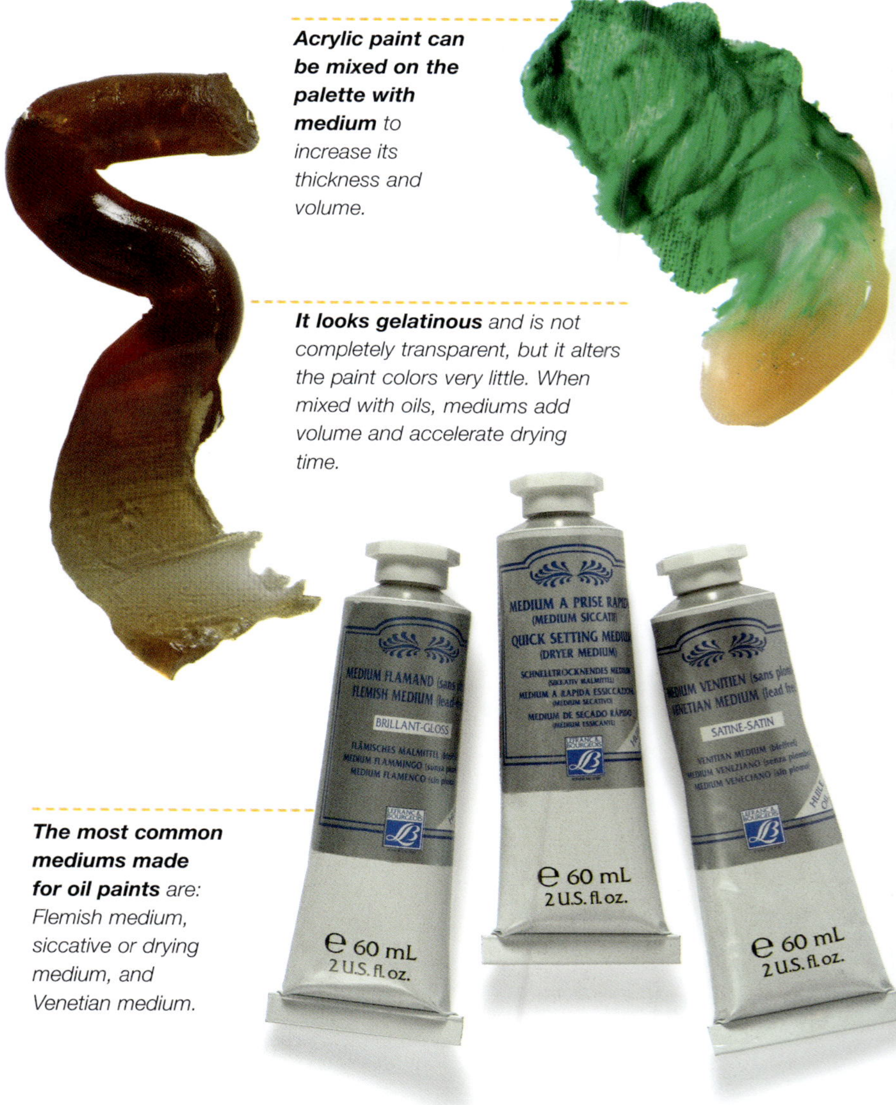

Acrylic paint can be mixed on the palette with medium *to increase its thickness and volume.*

It looks gelatinous *and is not completely transparent, but it alters the paint colors very little. When mixed with oils, mediums add volume and accelerate drying time.*

The most common mediums made for oil paints *are: Flemish medium, siccative or drying medium, and Venetian medium.*

Greater Volume and Viscosity

When creating a large format painting with oil or acrylic impastos, or with thick heavy brushstrokes, there is the option of adding gels or mediums to the paint to thicken it. They are a good alternative to wasting excessive paint. Mediums and gels change the volume and viscosity of the paint, which can be applied with brushes or spatulas once mixed. You must keep in mind that acrylics dry fast, so it is important to remember to keep your brushes in a container of water when they are not being used; otherwise the hair will harden in just a matter of minutes.

Gels and Mediums for Impasto

When working with acrylics it is common to add gels to the paint to increase its viscosity and even to enhance the durability of the brush marks. Obviously, with greater thickness impasto brushstrokes and spatula marks become more pronounced. There are also special gels for oils, which are known by the generic name oleopasto or impasto medium. The best ones are Flemish medium and Venetian medium. In oil painting, where the paint dries slowly, the addition of medium in the mixture accelerates the drying of the colors. Paintings that would require two weeks to dry can be ready in just a few days.

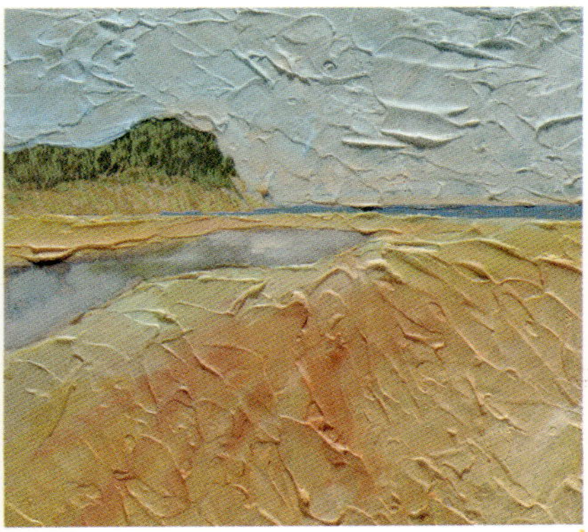

***Acrylic gel is consistent** and can be mixed directly with acrylics or prepared as a base which, after drying, can be painted over with oils.*

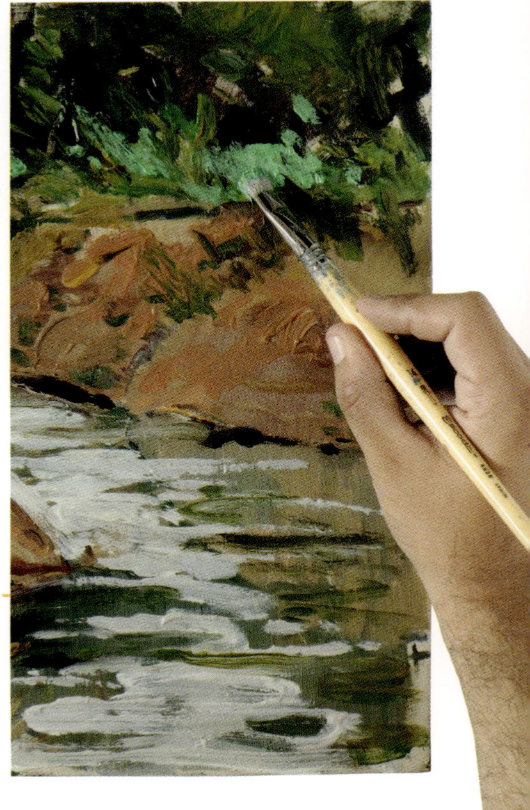

***The main disadvantage of oleopasto (or any other gel) is its light consistency.** Since it has no filler it usually flattens somewhat shortly after application.*

Modeling Paste

Modeling paste is denser and has more consistency than acrylic gels and mediums. It can be made from gesso or a mixture of natural or chemical resins to which filler is added. Each form of modeling paste or relief paste will create different effects.

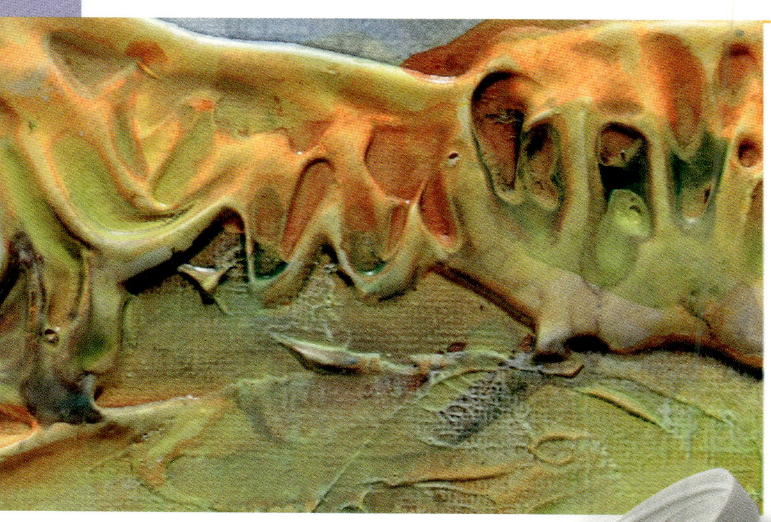

Gesso is probably the most common modeling paste. *It is white in color and easily applied to the support. After it has dried, it makes a very good surface for receiving any kind of paint.*

There are different forms of gesso, *from the lightest to the densest of gels. All of them have a fine texture and the paste can always be modeled with a metal spatula.*

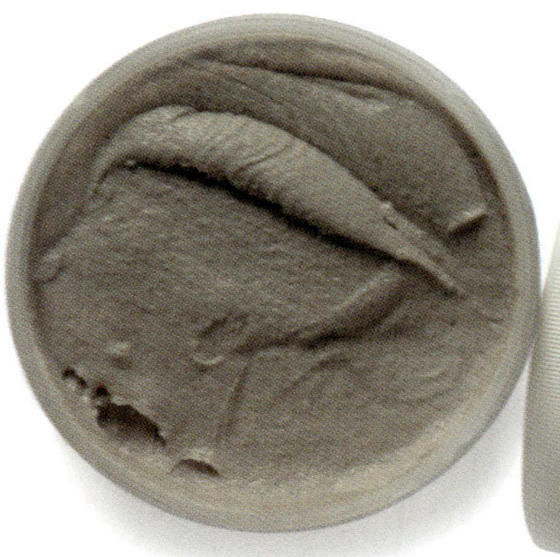

Modeling paste with a very fine texture *is best for working with a brush, preferably one with long hog hair bristles.*

Only with a Spatula

The modeling paste is a gel combined with a filler that usually consists of washed sand, marble dust, or other granulated products. The modeling paste is very suitable for impasto techniques with a spatula, but quite unsuitable for brush painting because the abrasiveness of the paste would destroy the hair of the hardest brush (mediums and gels are to be used in this case). Compared with the medium and the gel, its main advantage is its greater consistency, which allows us to create relief by modeling the surface with the spatula blade until all bas-relief effects become permanent.

Drying the Modeling Paste

When the paste is wet, it usually has a milky grey color that darkens during the drying stage. This is something to take into account when mixing transparent or clear colors. Since the acrylic medium dries by evaporation, the paste dries quickly and may be rigid in a few hours. Some artists speed up drying time by using a hair dryer or exposing the canvas to the sun. It is best to let it dry slowly, because a prolonged exposure to strong summer sunshine will dry the paste too fast and lead to crackling.

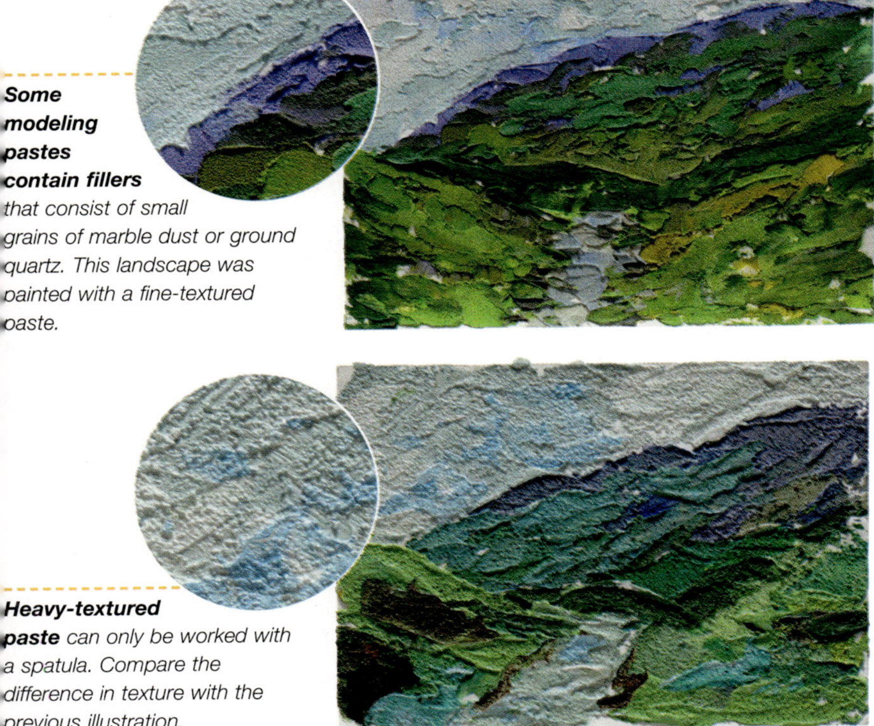

Some modeling pastes contain fillers *that consist of small grains of marble dust or ground quartz. This landscape was painted with a fine-textured paste.*

Heavy-textured paste *can only be worked with a spatula. Compare the difference in texture with the previous illustration.*

THE SUBJECT

Transparency with Textures

There is nothing like acrylics for work with transparencies—the results can be as bright and luminous as watercolors, and at the same time, as dense as oils. The combination of acrylic paint and gel medium creates a surface that can be textured and manipulated as long as it is wet.

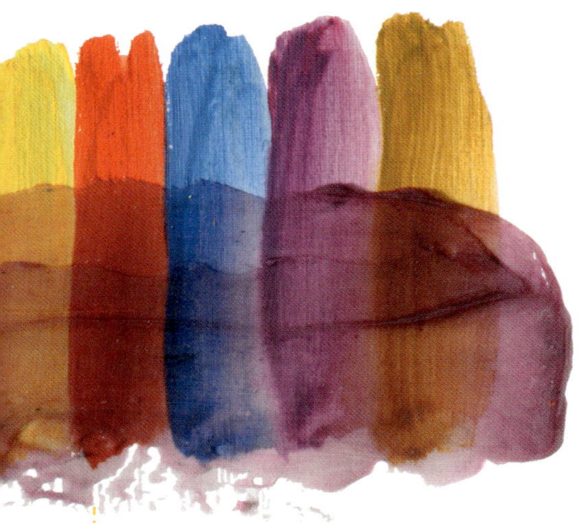

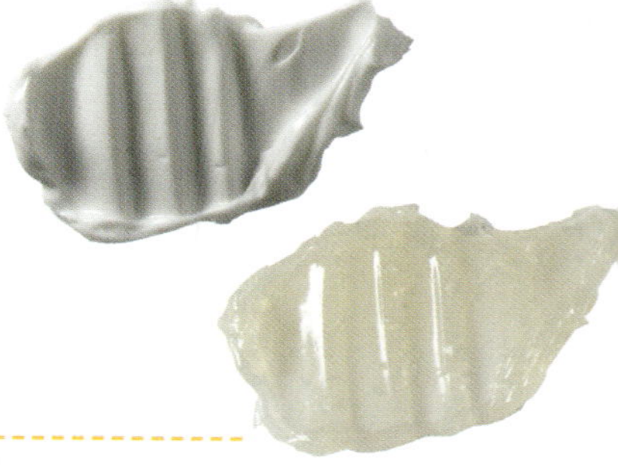

Acrylic gel is a white milky substance *that becomes transparent when it dries; it can be used to create transparent textures when mixed with a tiny amount of paint.*

Just like with watercolors, *a layer of gel tinted with violet, when dry, becomes transparent and alters the perception of the colors underneath; acts like a glaze of thick paint.*

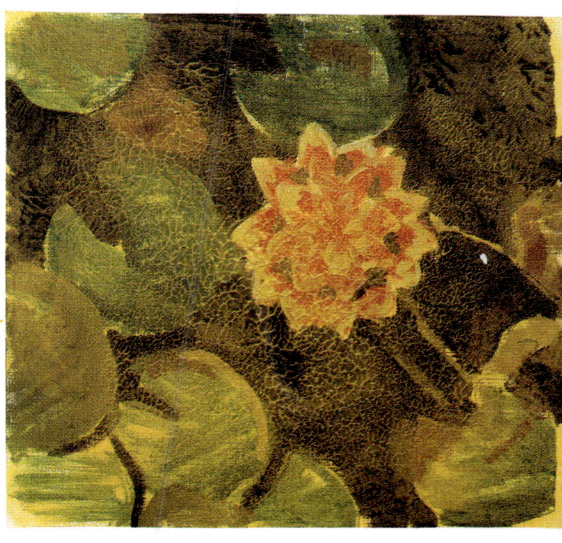

If you wish to change the final tones of the color in a painting, *and at the same time add a relief effect, you can paint a glaze with a translucent yellow impasto.*

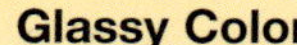

Like Watercolors with Body

Any amateur artist knows that watercolors are water-based mediums used to paint layers of color over each other, and that they cannot be used with relief techniques. However, the effect produced by painting transparencies with acrylics is exactly the same as that of watercolors, except that with acrylics the transparency can have some body. Mediums that have enough consistency for creating textures or impastos are only for acrylics; there are no similar substances for oils.

Glassy Color

A small amount of acrylic paint mixed with medium or transparent gel will create a stained glass effect. It can then be spread on a surface that has previously been painted. The underlying paint might be initially hidden by a very white and opaque layer, since some gels do not become transparent until they have completely dried. The gel will look like a layer of translucent paint tinted with the color that you have mixed previously.

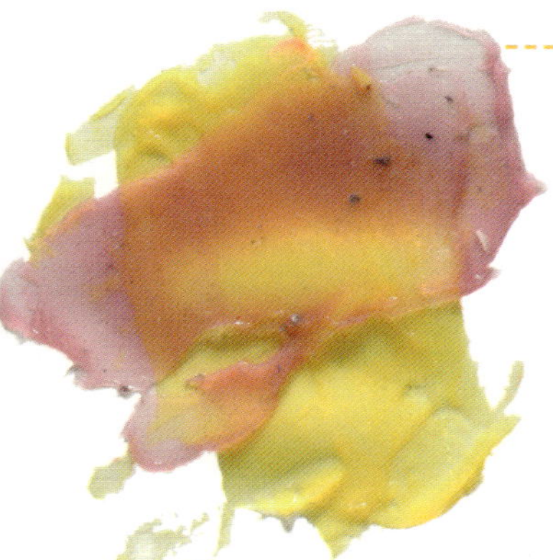

When working with transparent textures *the colors are created by overlaying glazes; each new addition of color affects those below it.*

Mix a small amount of color with a large amount of gel when painting. *It is very important to apply a great amount of gel to the support to create a good amount of volume. When first applied the gel is whitish, and you will not be able to see the final result of the applications until the paint is completely dry.*

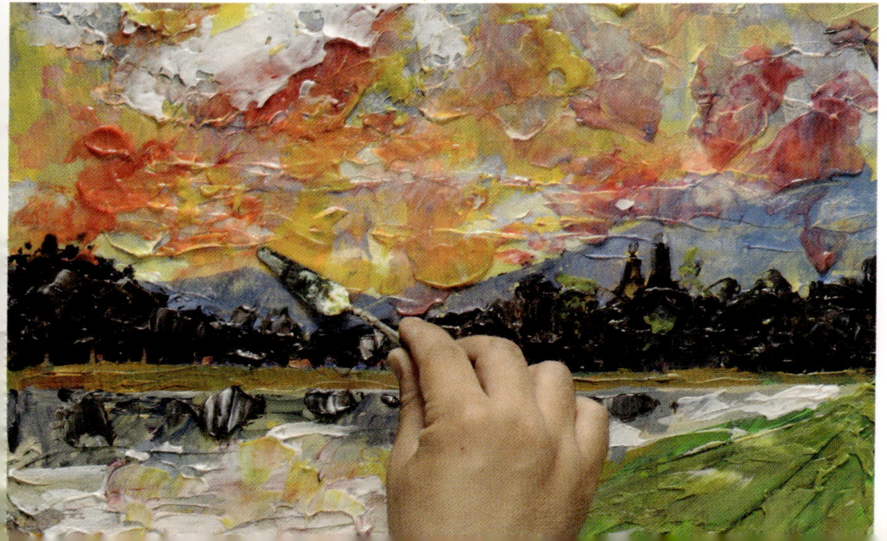

THE SUBJECT

Impasto with a Brush

The word "impasto" describes a painting that is applied in heavy layers, so that the brush marks can clearly be seen. The thickness of oil paint, and its stability after it has dried, makes it ideal for creating a painting with heavy brushstrokes. Impasto paintings are most commonly painted with oils—acrylics, though not as thick, can also be used to create interesting results.

Impastos are characterized by heavy, undiluted applications of paint. *Brushstrokes can be seen in the surface of the painting.*

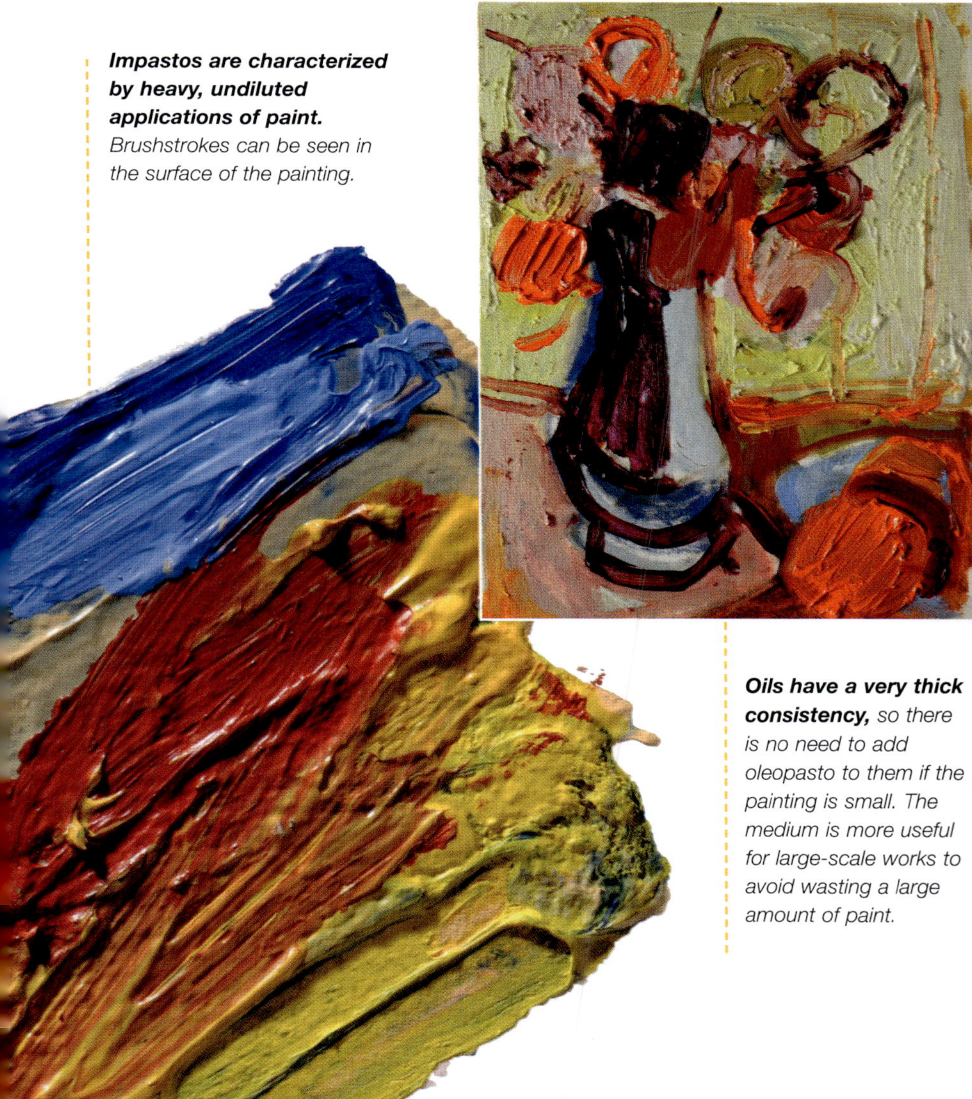

Oils have a very thick consistency, *so there is no need to add oleopasto to them if the painting is small. The medium is more useful for large-scale works to avoid wasting a large amount of paint.*

The Density of Oils

Impasto refers to the deposit of a certain amount of paint on a canvas with a brush with no attempt to spread it. You can use extremely thick impasto, made with the addition of oleopasto, to create a sculptural three-dimensional painting. Square, flat brushes are best for working on small-format impastos, because you can pick up the paint from the palette like a shovel and then apply a thick brushstroke. Impasto encourages relief and suggestive textures with the masses of paint. It has a significant physical presence and tends to "advance," so if you wish to maintain depth in a composition, the impasto should be reserved for the foreground or focal point.

Impastos with Acrylics

Acrylic paint has less volume and viscosity than oils, and its relief tends to shrink about thirty percent when it dries. When painting impastos, it is best to mix acrylics with heavy gel since paint straight from the tube has little consistency. By adding gel to the acrylic paint it becomes more malleable and dense enough to preserve the stroke and brush marks.

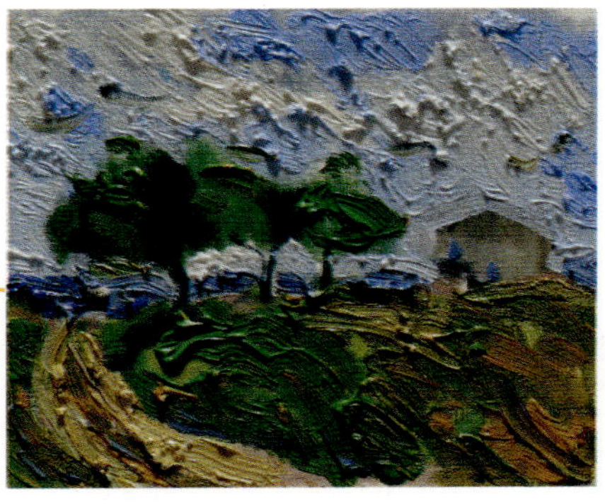

An impasto brushstroke on a landscape adds a strongly expressive component to the representation. *Therefore it is important not to use random brushstrokes, but to follow the direction of the terrain.*

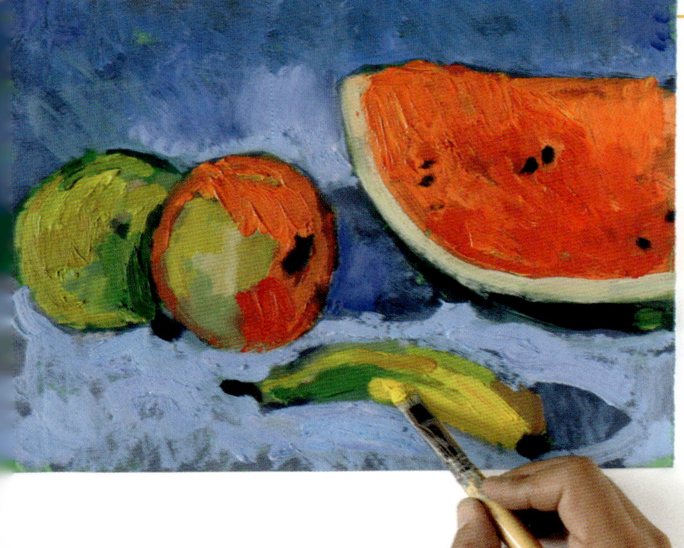

The impasto brushstrokes are used to create a false illusion of relief on the surface of the objects. *The color has body and it shapes each element so that it advances towards the viewer. The relief pushes it out of the painting.*

THE SUBJECT

Impasto with a Spatula

The painter's spatula is a fundamental tool when it comes to relief painting. Many artists use it for spreading the paint across the surface and partially scraping it with the tip of the blade, or for creating different texture and relief effects. The secret of painting with a spatula is working with sureness and confidence, spreading the paint with large strokes of the hand.

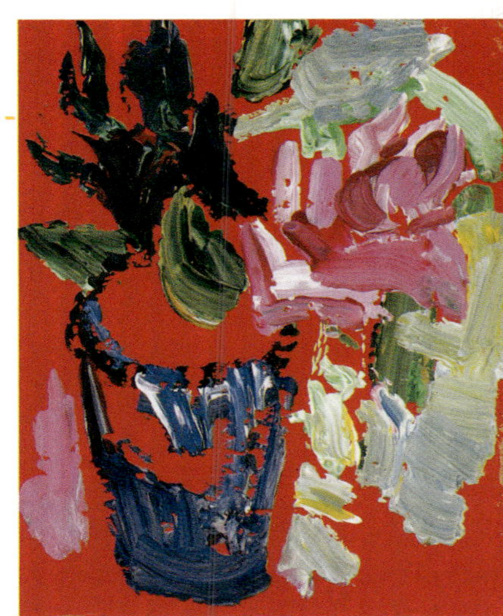

When working with a spatula it is better to apply the impasto in a stylistic way, *using the textures creatively instead of trying to be true to reality.*

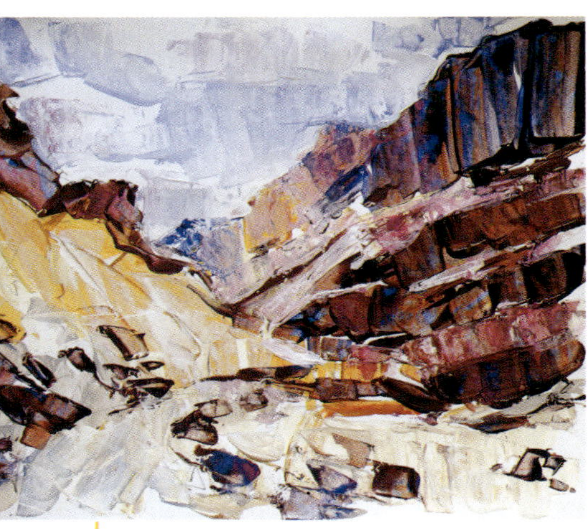

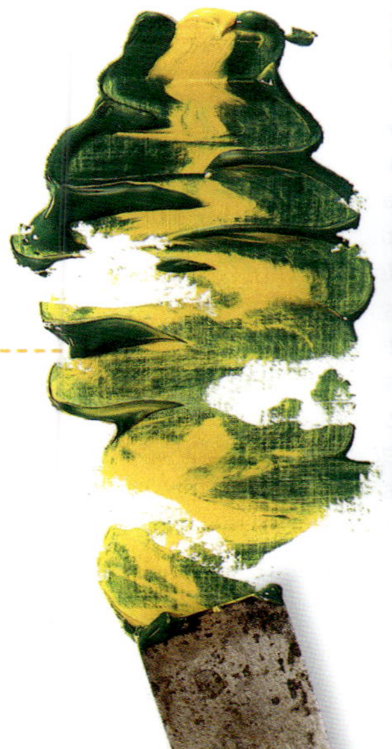

There are many types of painting spatulas, *although you can even use a plasterer's spatula or a putty knife. These can be very useful when painting a large-format work.*

Painting impastos with a putty knife *allows you to concentrate on constructing a painting based on well-structured masses and ignoring the details.*

Applying Paint

Painting with a spatula can seem more complicated than painting with a brush, so it is a good idea to practice until you have developed some skill. The spatula is not moved back and forth as if it were a brush. You pick up the paint with the back of the blade and the widest part is used to spread it on the surface with a single bold motion, cleanly lifting the blade when the stroke is complete. You should apply the paint holding the spatula at different angles, changing the amount that the blade is tipped to create different strokes and effects.

Spatulas and Their Effects

Long flat blades are flexible and ideal for applying large areas of color. Smaller diamond-shaped ones are better for small-format paintings and for applying controlled strokes. Spatulas with flat tips let you make impasto applications that are small and rectangular, almost like working with a square tip brush. Plastic spatulas are not recommended because they are not very flexible and they do not easily return to their original shape when bent. A medium can be used to give more body to the impasto: heavy gel medium if you are working with acrylics, and oleopasto if you are painting with oils. These mediums thicken the paint without altering its color; they also make it stretch a long way and they accelerate the drying time.

The painter's spatula allows greater variety in the application of impasto. *The hand is freer to change direction and give shape to the creamy paint that is applied to the canvas. A slight touch or twist of the wrist is enough to suggest a bush.*

Any surface with oil impasto applied using a painter's spatula is spectacular. *The strokes, the broken texture, and the accumulated paint create a very attractive relief surface with a strong visual impact.*

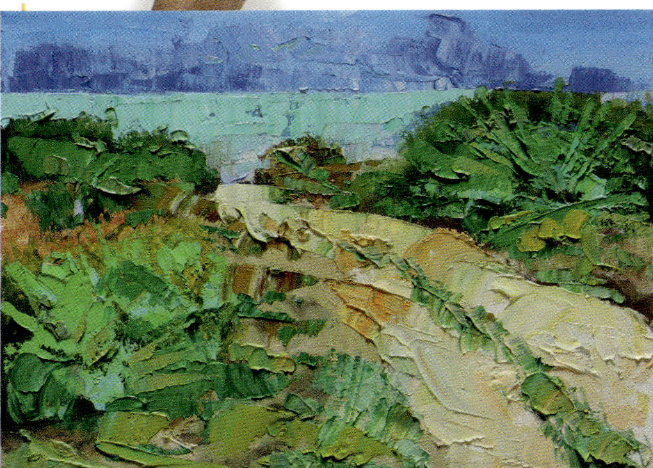

IN THE STYLE OF...

Oskar Kokoschka (1886–1980)

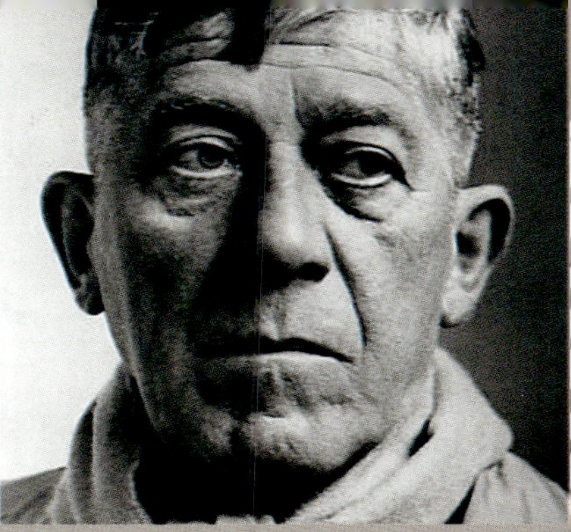

Kokoschka knew how to channel his tormented personality into the nervous brushstroke that was characteristic of his paintings.

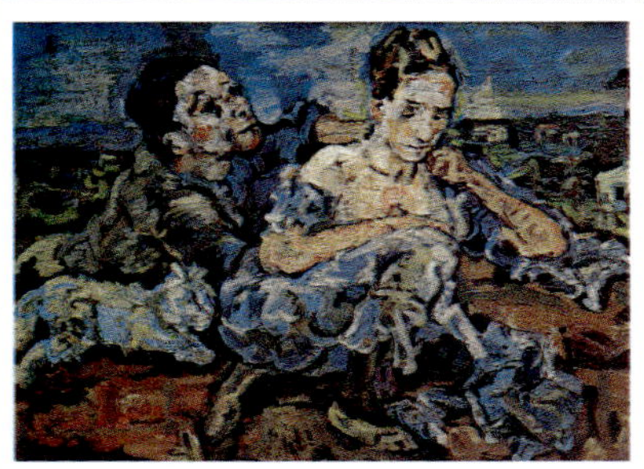

Lovers with Cat *(1917).*
At the end of his life, Kokoschka paints with bands of paint that gradually become thicker, heavier, and intertwined, giving the impression that the figures are melting. The brushstroke, which becomes increasingly voluminous, gives the surface a feeling of movement and conveys a sense of anguished restlessness to the painting. His oil paintings are constructed with a series of rounded and broken brushstrokes, through which the colors of the painting seem to be broken up.

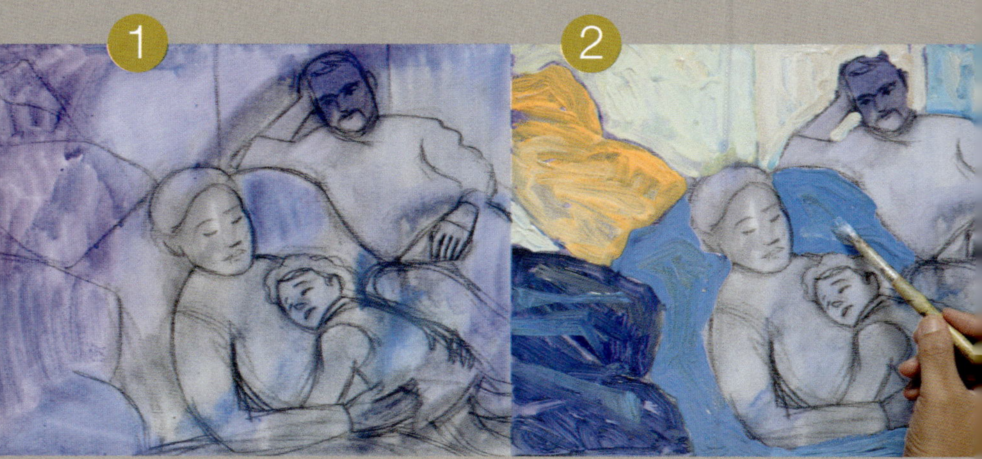

1. *Gabriel Martín will try to replicate Kokoschka's technique using oil paints. First, he does a pencil drawing of a group of figures and covers the background with blue paint mixed with turpentine.*

2. *The oil paints are mixed with oleopasto medium to give them more body and volume. He paints each area with a uniform color, but with very thick paint.*

An Austrian painter and poet, he was considered one of the main representatives of Expressionism in his country. His work was originally influenced by Jugendstil and, in a very direct way, by the painter Gustav Klimt. Gradually, however, his palette turned grayer and his brushstroke became more energetic, independent, and agitated. During his later years his paint was thicker and grayer, and he did not bother balancing the glossiness of the saturated colors, as the French and German Expressionists did in their paintings.

3. The artist applies nervous brushstrokes of thick paint in each area. The movement of the hand, the impulsive brushstroke, and the mixture of thick colors are all very important.

4. The brushstrokes are applied in different directions. The faces of the figures seem blurred while the background consists of juxtaposed lines, giving the painting an unusual feeling of restlessness.

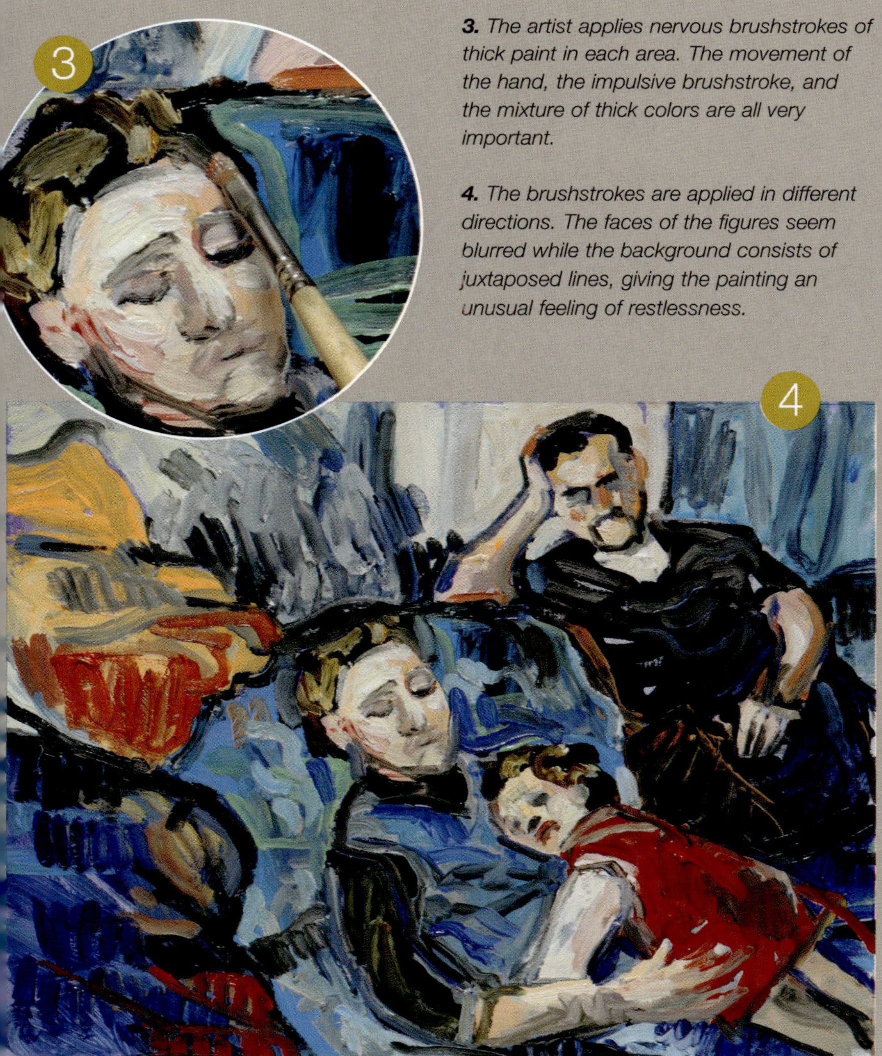

Adding Fillers to Paint

Fillers are inert additives that do not color the medium and whose only purpose is to create effects of texture. A filler can be any powder or small material that is added to oil and acrylic paints to change the texture of the paint and to give it more volume. If you use fillers, you should take some precautions: avoid any organic materials that can decompose, as well as chemicals and salts because they will eventually cause the support to deteriorate.

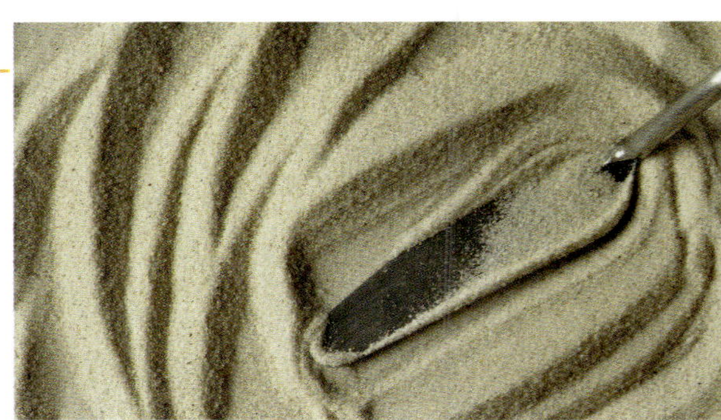

Fine sand is perhaps the most common filler because it is readily available. *The best kind is finely pulverized quartz.*

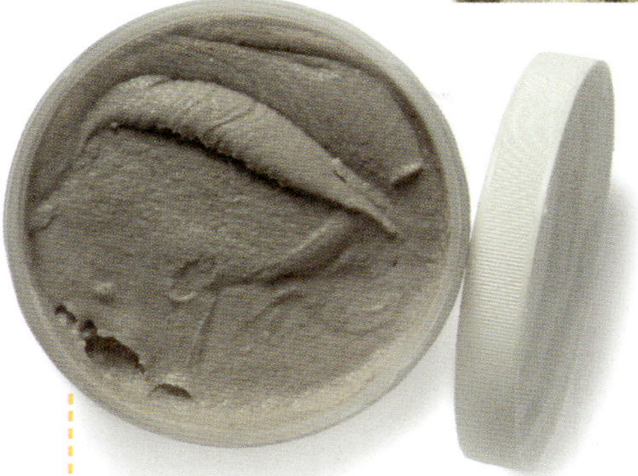

Art supply stores sell fillers that are already mixed *with an acrylic base, ready to be added to the paint. Here is a gel textured with fine marble dust.*

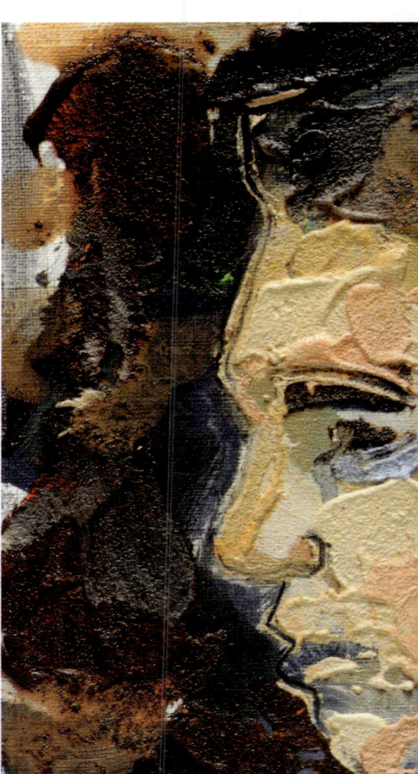

Pulverized Material and Paint

Fillers are solid elements that are finely pulverized and added to paint, whether combined with some medium or added directly. Fillers should be mixed into the paint thoroughly so they become part of it. Slight variations and light areas in the final mix are unavoidable. Fillers adhere to the paint when it dries, and any pulverized material that is mixed into the paint becomes part of it, thanks to the adhesive effect of the acrylic resin or linseed oil.

Considerations for the Mix

To incorporate fillers into acrylic paint, it is a good idea to dampen them first with latex or with an acrylic medium. But with oil paints, acrylic resins are not recommended since they do not mix well with them. In these cases, you can add a small amount of Dutch varnish or oleopasto. The filler (fine sand, marble dust, or carborundum) can be added as needed. Do not saturate the medium, since too much filler can overwhelm the paint completely and prevent it from adhering to the support. The mixture should be thick; otherwise the filler will settle to the bottom of the container.

Fillers can be mixed directly with acrylics *and applied with a spatula. They will dry in just a few minutes.*

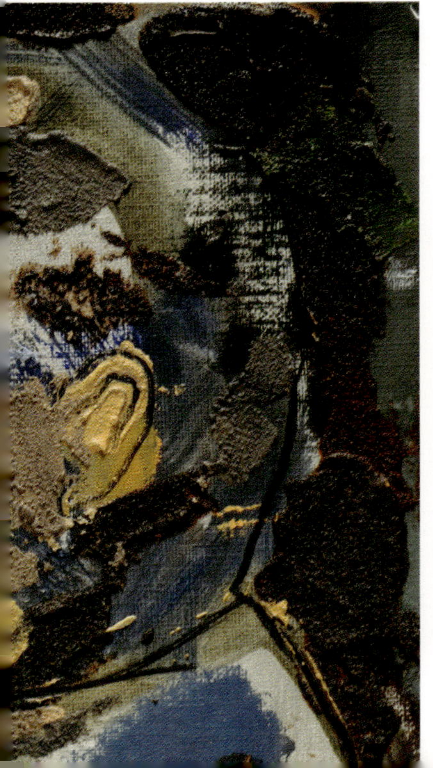

Textured gel cannot be mixed directly with oil paint; *it is better to paint over the gel when it is completely dry. There is another option: mix the filler with oil paste.*

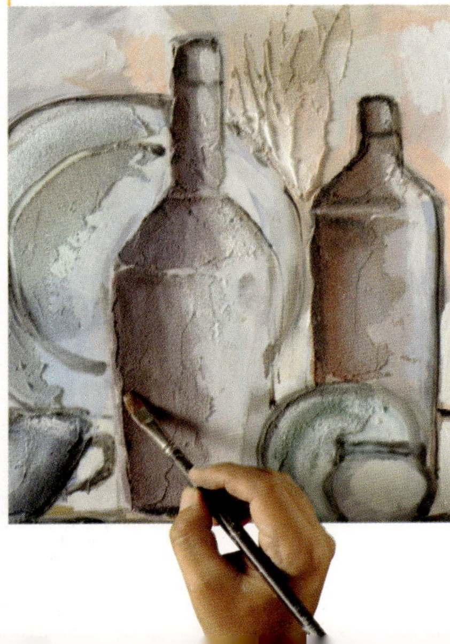

LET'S EXPERIMENT

Landscape with Acrylics and a Spatula

A field of sunflowers, which gives this landscape its characteristic yellow color, is the inspiration for this exercise.

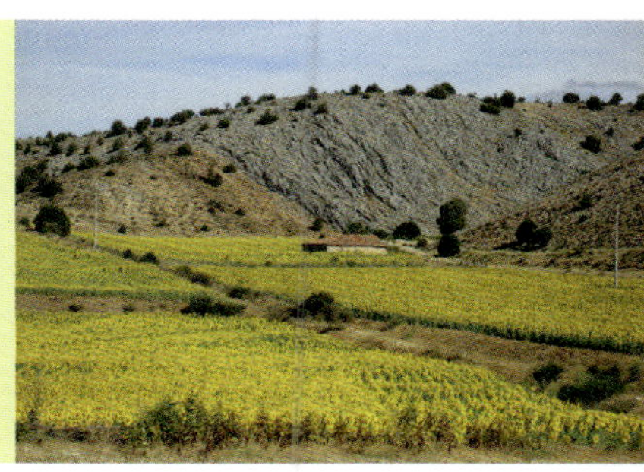

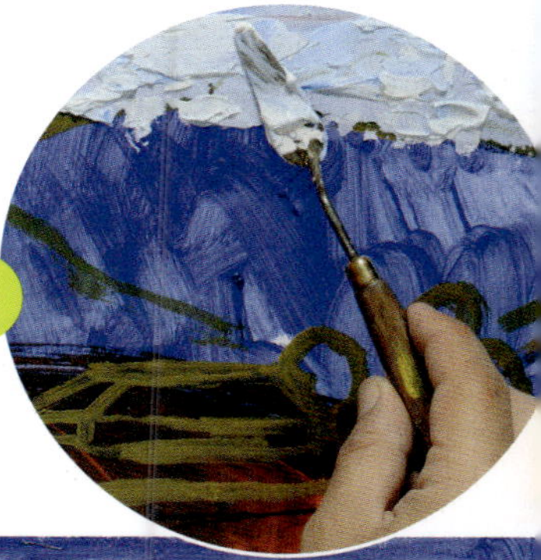

***1.** Cover the white canvas using very diluted acrylic paint. Paint the bottom half red and the top half ultramarine blue. This is the background over which you are going to paint.*

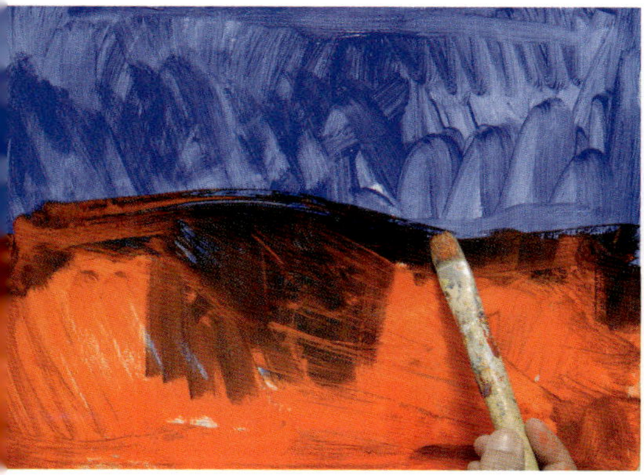

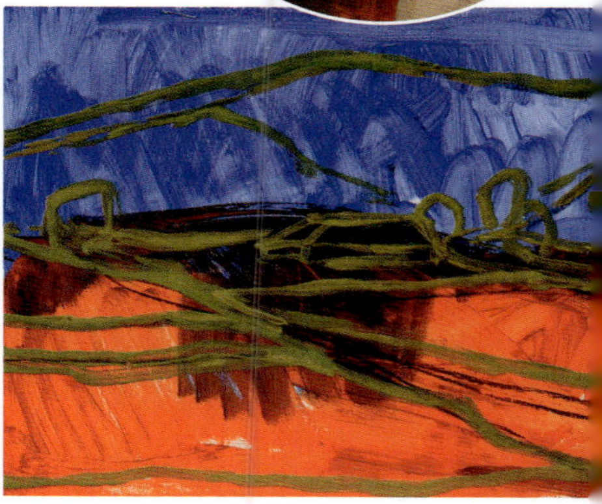

1

2

3

***2.** Apply the paint in layers no thicker than 1/4 inch (6 mm), and let it dry before you add the next layer. If the layers are too thick, the paint on top will dry faster than the paint underneath, causing the surface to crack.*

***3.** On the palette mix a small amount of blue with a generous amount of gesso. Pick it up with the spatula and apply it over the sky. By adding a touch of crimson, the color will turn slightly more violet. This is how small variations are created.*

This landscape has been created with acrylic paints and a spatula. As a variation, gesso, which is normally used for priming, has been added to the paint as if it were a filler. This gives more volume and opacity to the acrylic paint. This method has pros and cons: with gesso, acrylic paints have better body and consistency when applied with a spatula; however, they do not become transparent when dry like they would when mixed with gels. This means that the mixture of gesso and acrylic paint tends to make colors look whiter.

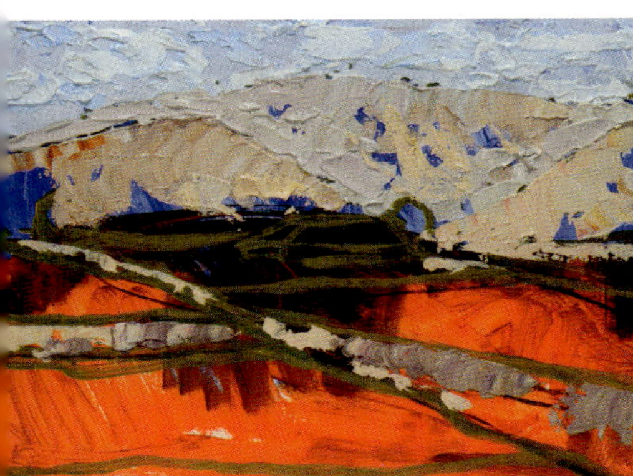

***4.** Prepare another batch of violet and orange. Again, mix it on the palette with a generous amount of gesso. Apply a thick layer over the mountains in the background.*

4

5

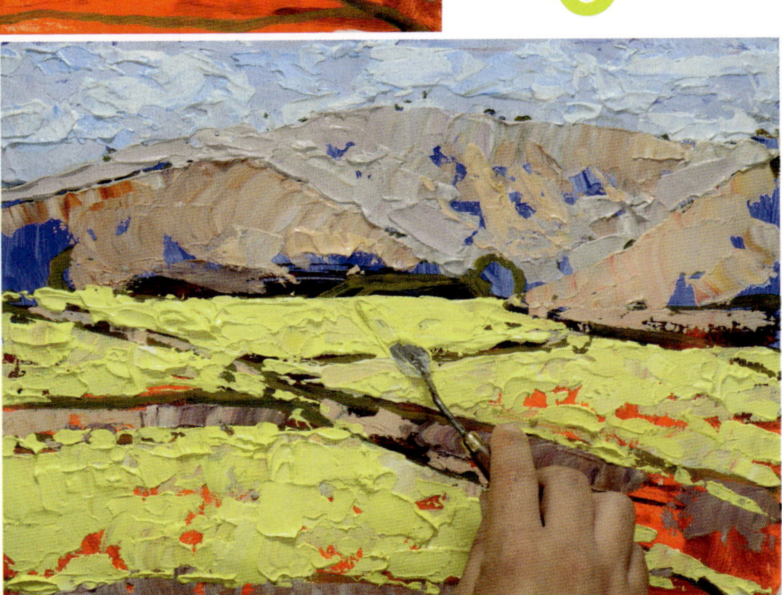

***5.** The goal is to apply a layer of various colors to cover the surface, leaving a few areas unpainted through which the initial base colors will peek through.*

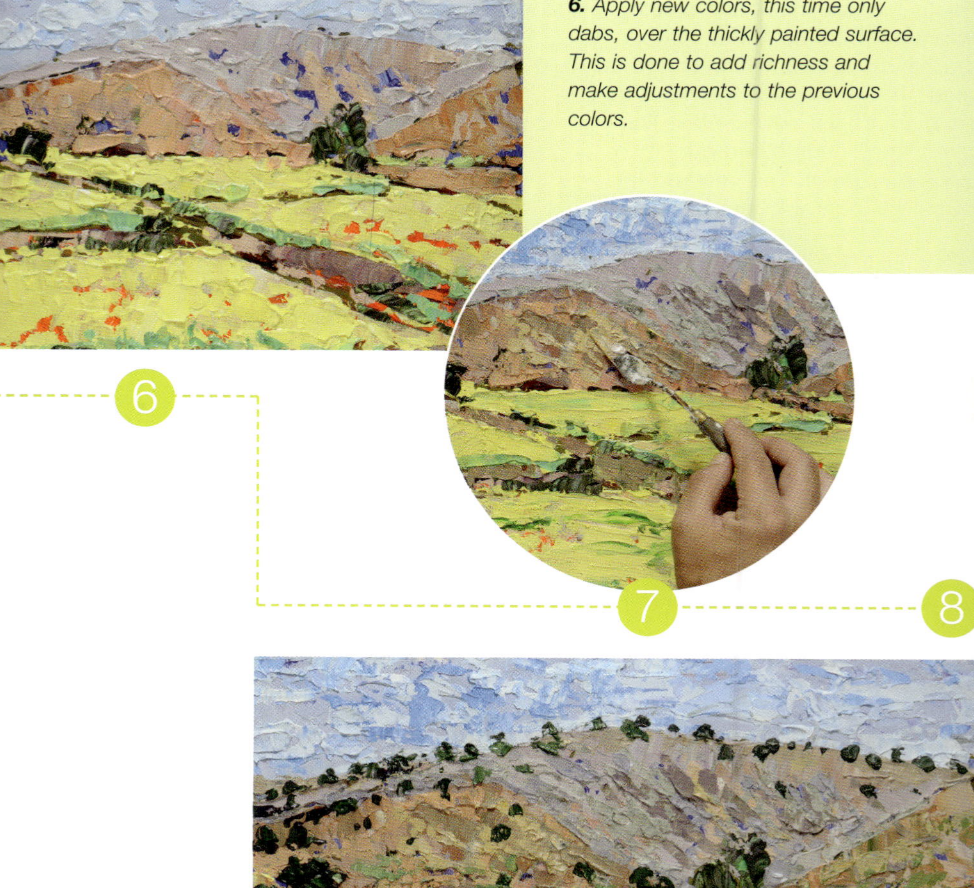

6. *Apply new colors, this time only dabs, over the thickly painted surface. This is done to add richness and make adjustments to the previous colors.*

7. *Angle the spatula according to the surface you are working on; use the flat side of the blade over the fields, and angle it diagonally for the mountains and treetops.*

8. *With the tip of the round spatula outline the trees and the bushes. Apply thick paint again, this time brighter yellow, over the fields of flowers.*

__9.__ Since it is not possible to apply details with a spatula, use a thin round brush to paint the house. You only need four colors to define it.

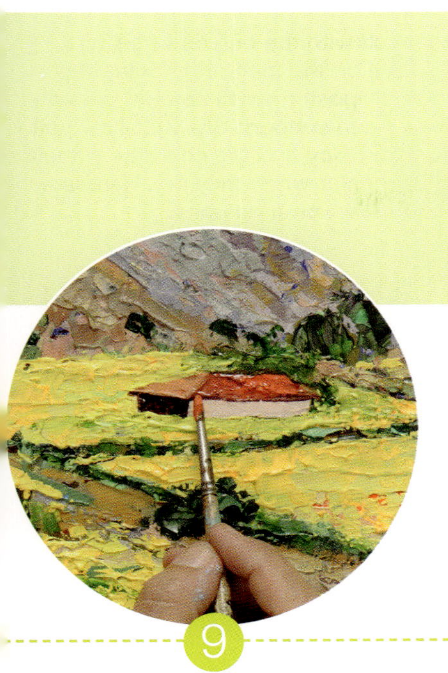

__10.__ The last touch-ups are done with acrylic paints, without gesso. Gabriel Martín uses this approach to brighten the final colors and prevent the composition from looking too washed out.

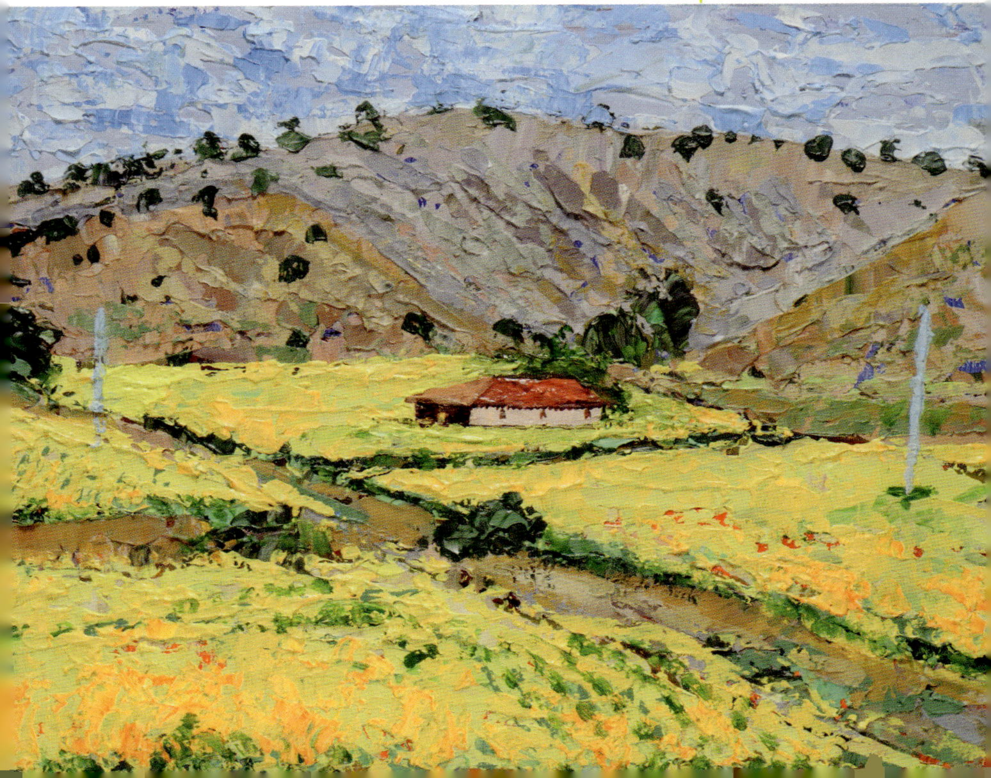

All About Gels and Mediums

Familiarize yourself with the different gels and mediums available on the market by doing this simple exercise. Deposit a small amount of each substance on a white support; this will allow you to test their consistency and the changes in their transparency and color when they dry. Here is a selection of the most common ones.

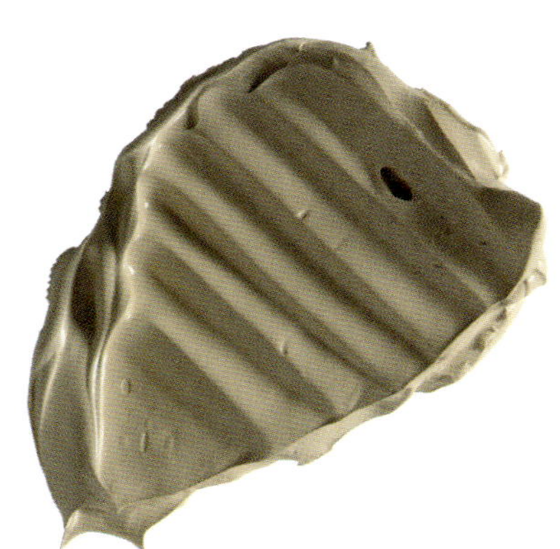

Pink gesso. This variety is preferred by painters who like to use that color base.

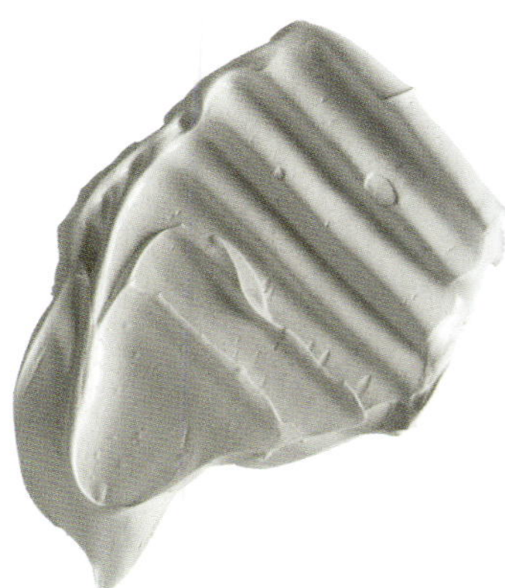

Extra heavy gesso. It is heavier and has more weight than conventional gesso. It is also easier to manipulate.

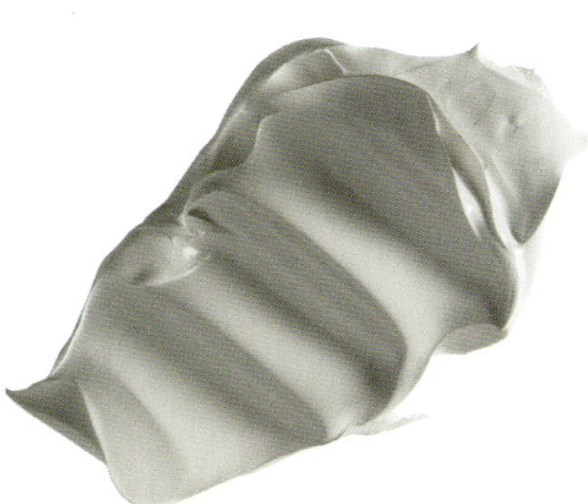

Super strong gesso. Very similar to the previous example, but with added adhesive strength. It sets harder and stronger when it dries.

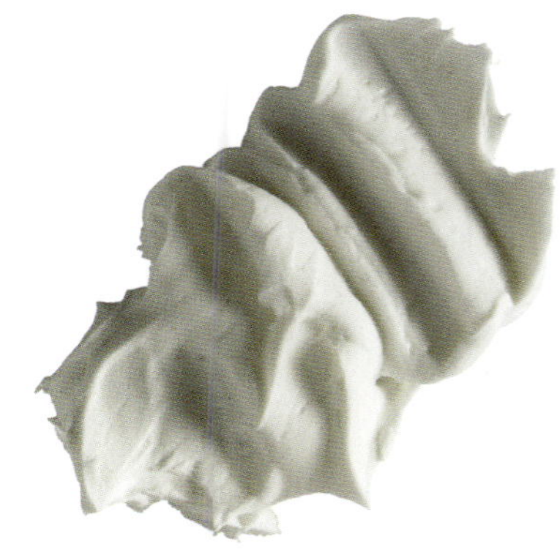

Light modeling paste. This has more volume than gesso and is easier to work with a spatula. It maintains its white color after it dries.

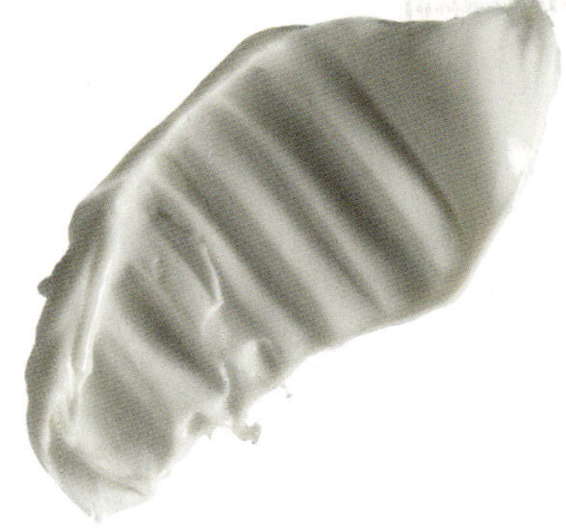

Glossy thick gesso. It has less consistency than the previous one. It loses part of its volume and turns completely transparent when it dries.

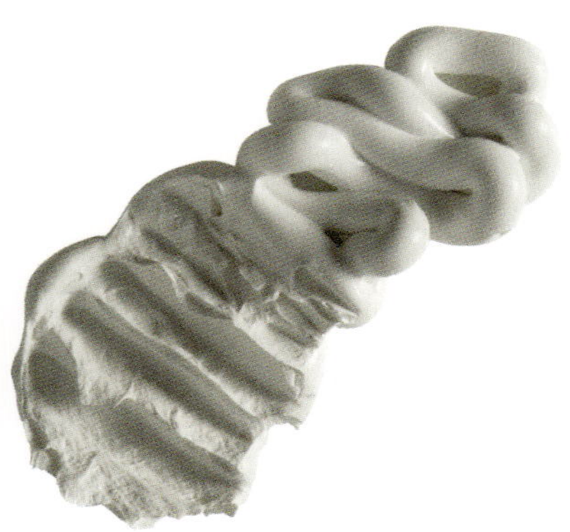

Titan heavy gel. This gel provides volume and consistency. It maintains its white color after it dries.

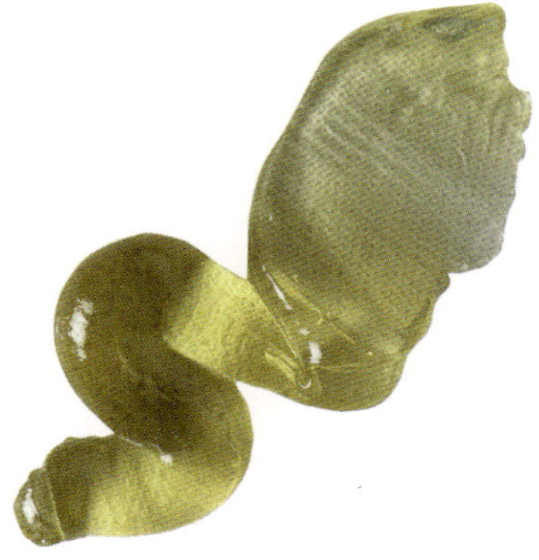

Drying medium for oils. In addition to providing volume it dramatically speeds up the drying process. It becomes completely transparent when it dries.

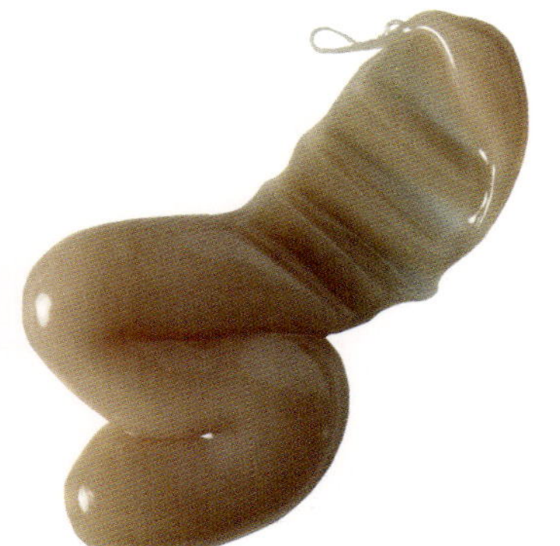

Oleopasto. It is the most suitable gel for oil paints. It increases the volume of the paint, but it also reduces its solidity and firmness. It becomes more translucent after it dries.

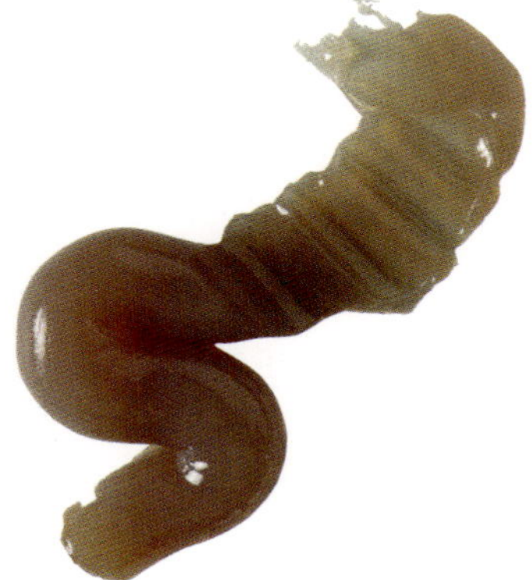

Liquin impasto. It has characteristics similar to oleopastos, although it has greater consistency. In addition to adding volume to the oils, it speeds up their drying time.

Modeling with a Spatula

A spatula is a flexible metal blade that the artist can use as a scoop. You can spread and model any creamy and consistent substance with it on the surface of the canvas to give it any desired shape. This allows you to create smooth effects, layered areas, or patterns that would be otherwise impossible to create with a brush.

With the back of the spatula *you can create smooth surfaces.*

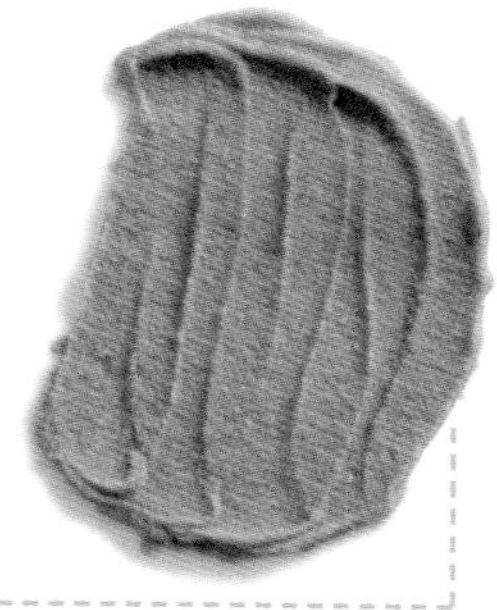

With a slight zigzag movement *of the hand you can create layers and striations.*

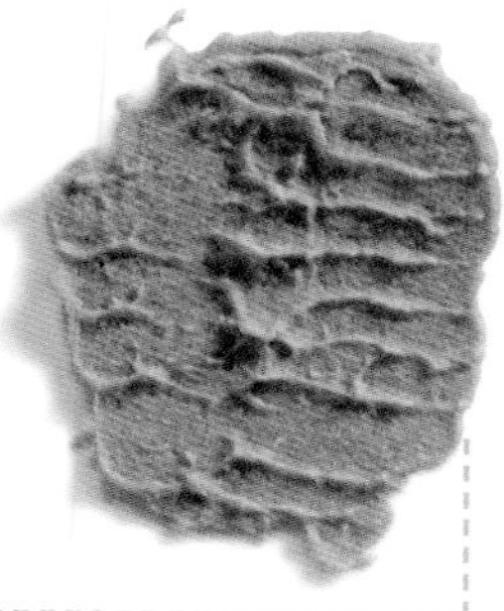

By simply pressing and then lifting the blade of the spatula *you can texture the gel.*

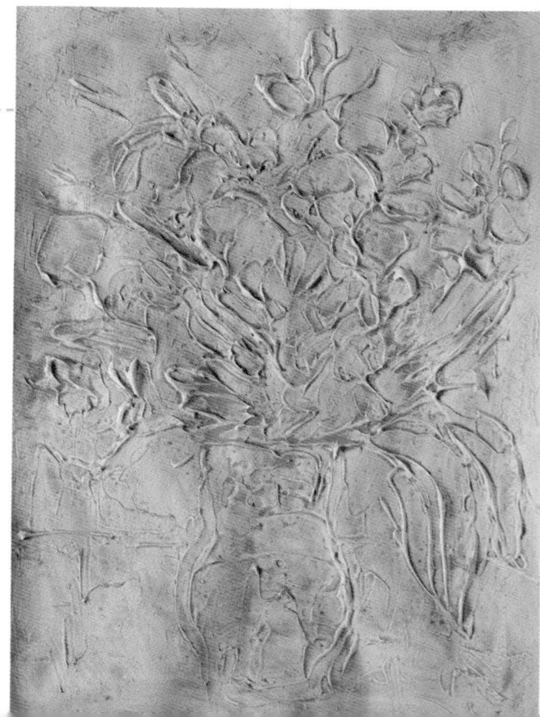

By modeling the gesso with a spatula *you can obtain three-dimensional images, as if it were a bas-relief.*

Dealing with a Bas-Relief

When you plan to cover the surface of the support with large amounts of gesso, gel, or modeling paste, applying them with a brush can be difficult. Instead, you should spread these substances with a medium or large round-tip spatula. A spatula allows you to extend the paste evenly over the entire support. Furrows, valleys, peaks, and layers can be created by simply dragging the gesso from side to side. You need to prepare the surface relief before you begin to paint, as if you were creating a bas-relief of the model that you wish to create.

Different Textures

There are many modeling approaches that you can use with the spatula; simply take the spatula and experiment with it practicing different hand movements over gesso or thin textured gel. Depending on the movement and the pressure you apply, the blade will produce different types of textures on the surface. To familiarize yourself with them you can test different patterns on a piece of paper or board. Then you can combine the most attractive textures and effects on the final painting.

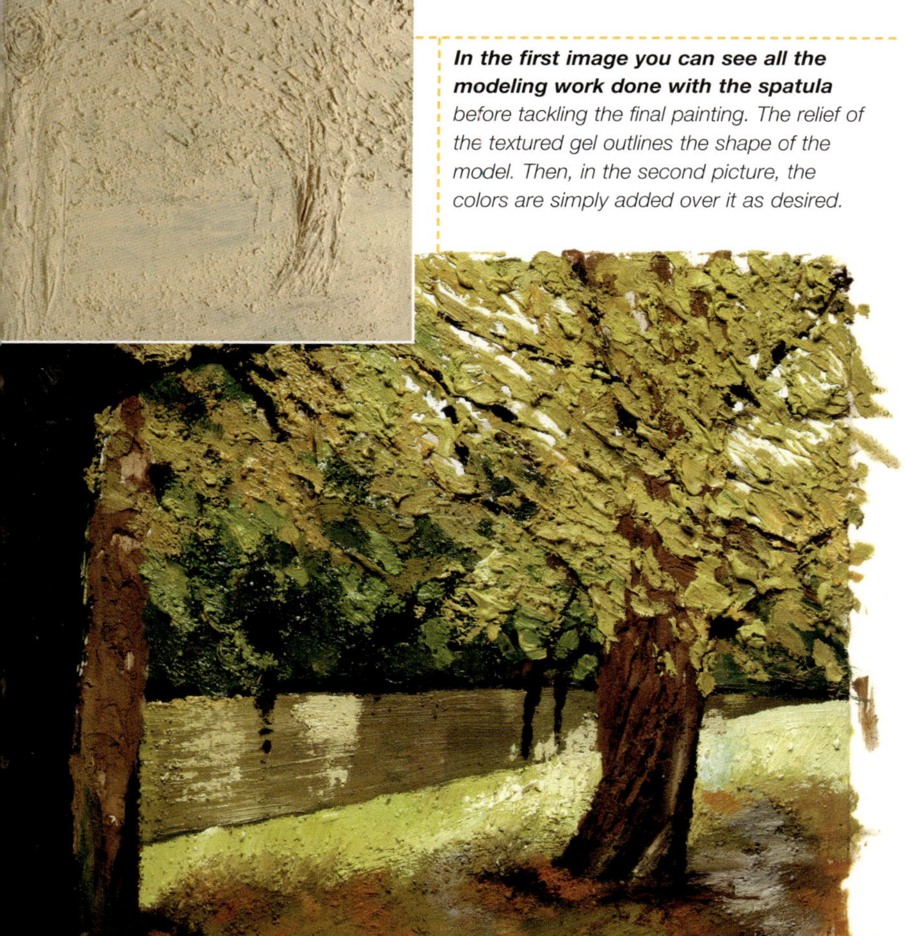

In the first image you can see all the modeling work done with the spatula *before tackling the final painting. The relief of the textured gel outlines the shape of the model. Then, in the second picture, the colors are simply added over it as desired.*

LET'S EXPERIMENT

Oils over Modeling Paste

Here is a colorful market scene, a good excuse for combining an urban landscape, a still life with fruit, and the human figure.

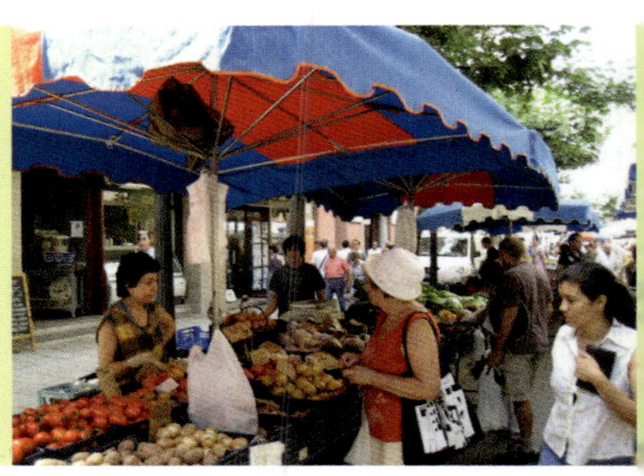

1. *Over a pencil drawing apply a generous amount of gesso with a round-tip metal spatula.*

2. *Spread the gesso without hesitation. You should attempt to recreate the scene with the modeled paste as if it were a bas-relief made of plaster.*

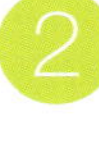

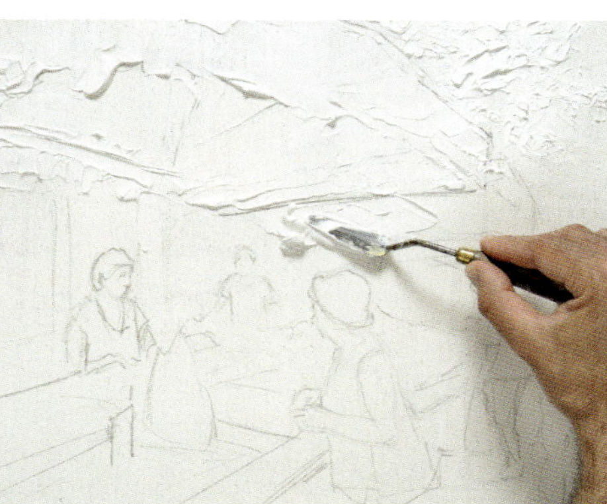

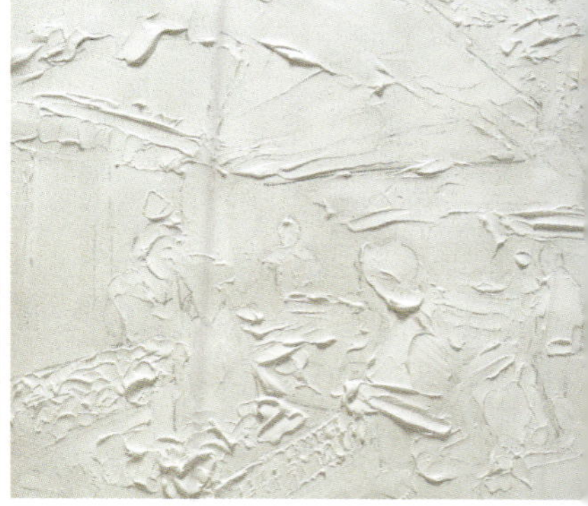

A VERY STRIKING RELIE

In a previous exercise we mixed gesso with acrylic paints. This time, the artist, Óscar Sanchís, combines the extra heavy modeling paste with oil paints. Do not mix the wet modeling paste with oils, because it has an acrylic base that is not compatible with oil base paints. Prepare the base first, wait until it dries and then paint over it. This way, the relief effect will be very striking and you will also conserve a lot of paint.

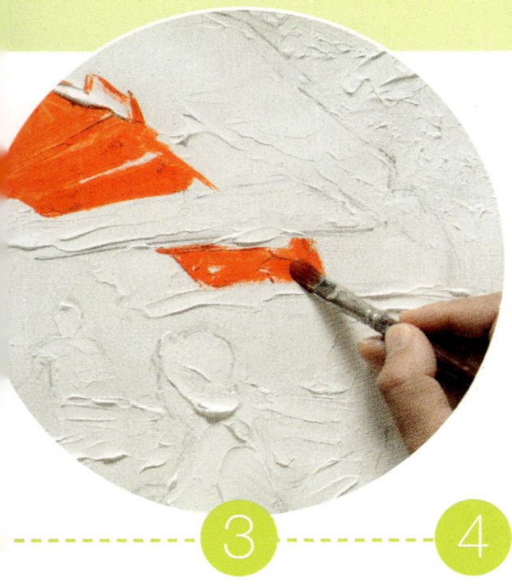

3. *You must wait at least a day for the gesso to dry. Paint with oils using bristle brushes, beginning with the umbrellas.*

4. *During these first phases, the paint can be diluted with a little bit of turpentine to allow the brush to flow better, especially if you take into account that you are painting over a surface with a very deep relief full of sharp edges.*

3 4 5

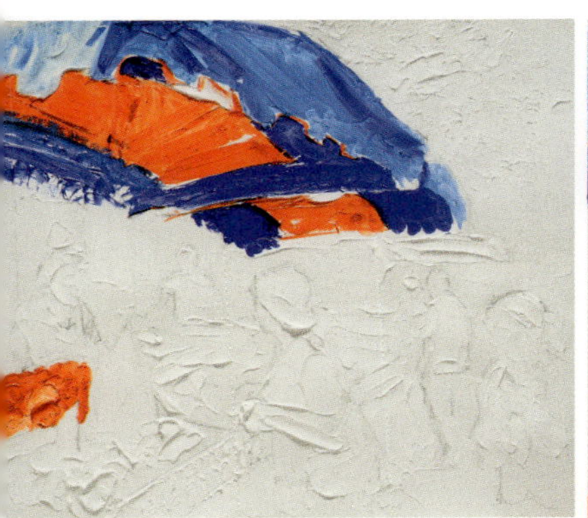

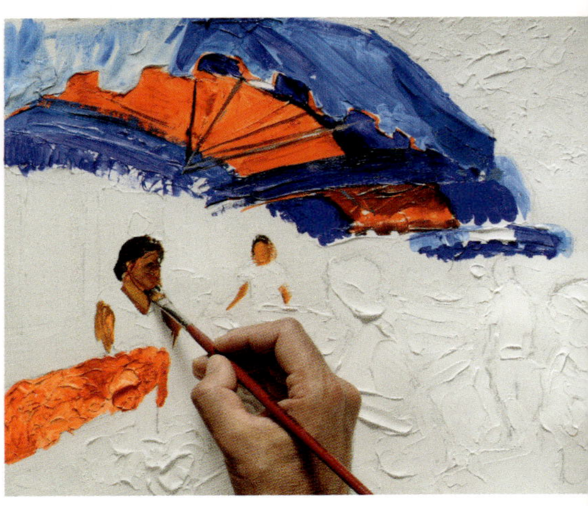

FFECT

5. *Work* alla prima, *which means that each area will be painted with only a few brushstrokes, mixing some of the colors directly on the surface of the painting.*

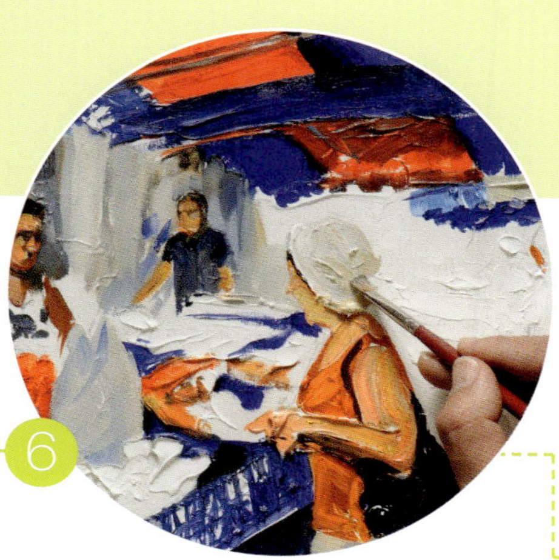

6. *Finer brushes are not only used for creating details but also for touching up or painting smaller areas. Such a heavily textured surface makes painting details difficult.*

7. *The figures and the market stand are merely suggested, almost like a sketch. The colors should coincide with the relief forms created at the beginning.*

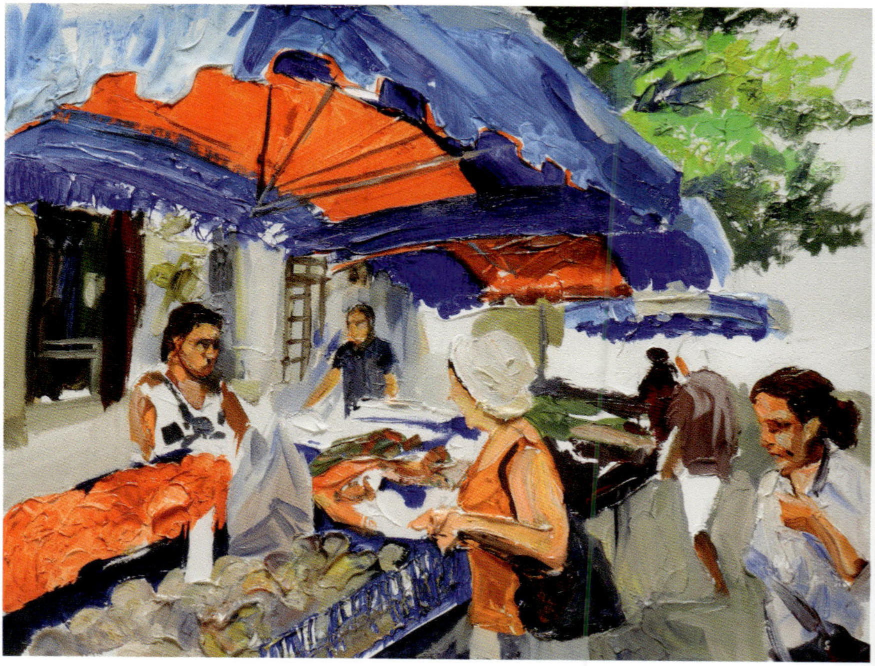

__8.__ Do not try to paint the fruit, simply add several touches of color. The high and low relief in the surface of the gesso make it impossible to paint a form with too much precision.

__9.__ The vegetation in the background is just suggested; there are even certain areas of the canvas that still have the original white color. The modeling paste painted over with oils provides a whimsical final effect that is spontaneous and very expressive.

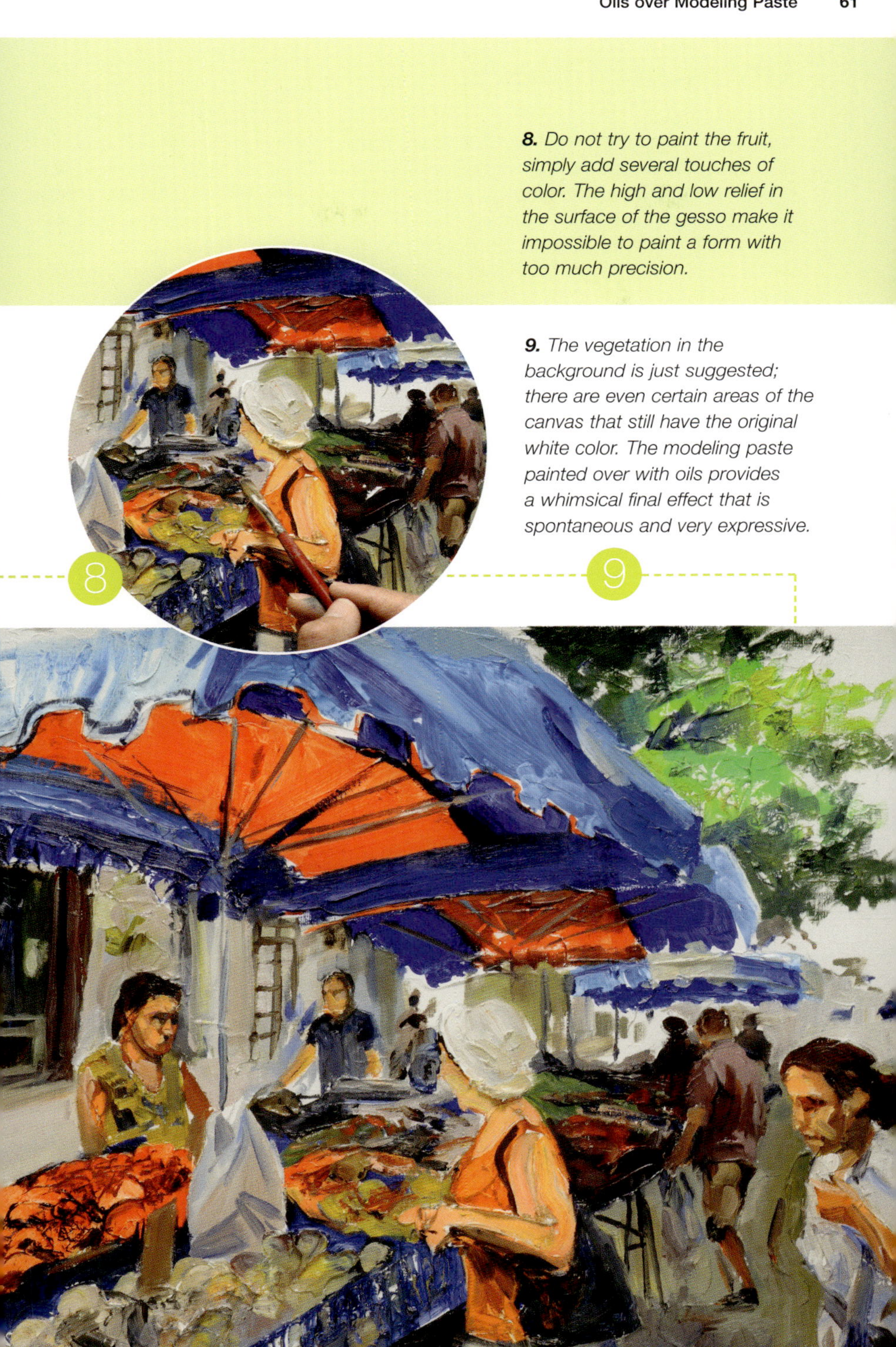

THE SUBJECT

Unusual Fillers

New types of pastes that contain fillers made of different materials are becoming available on the market all the time. They are very appealing for artists who are looking for new vibrant and energetic effects. Acrylic pastes are thickened with very unusual fillers that change the color of the texture and modify the way light is distributed on the support. These pastes are water-based; therefore they can be mixed with acrylics, and when they dry, they can be painted with oils as well.

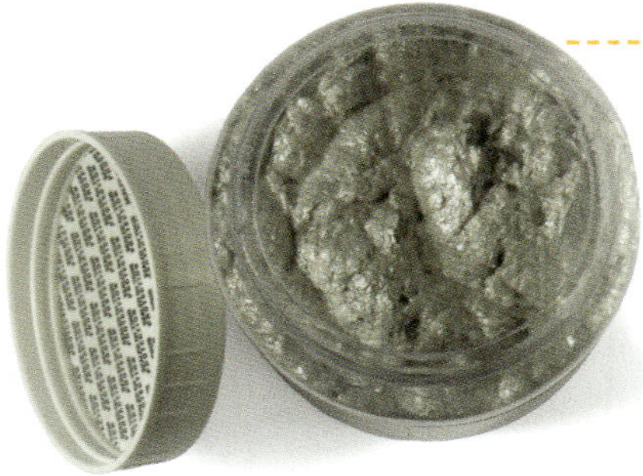

Acrylic base mixed with small particles of mica. *The resulting gel has a grayish texture and a very unique shiny silver tone.*

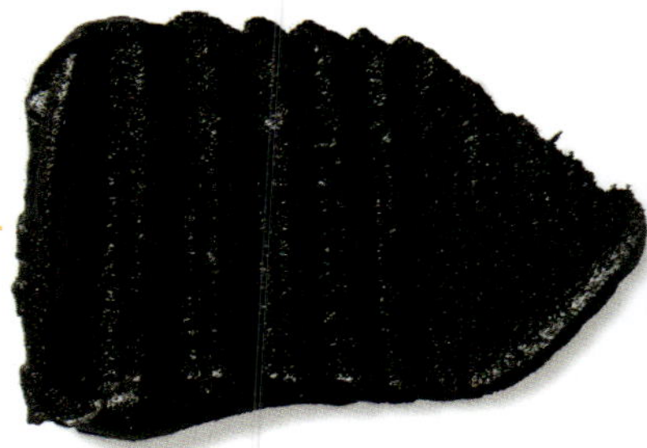

Black lava provides medium grain texture and dark color. *In the old days it used to be real powdered black lava, but these days an imitation is used.*

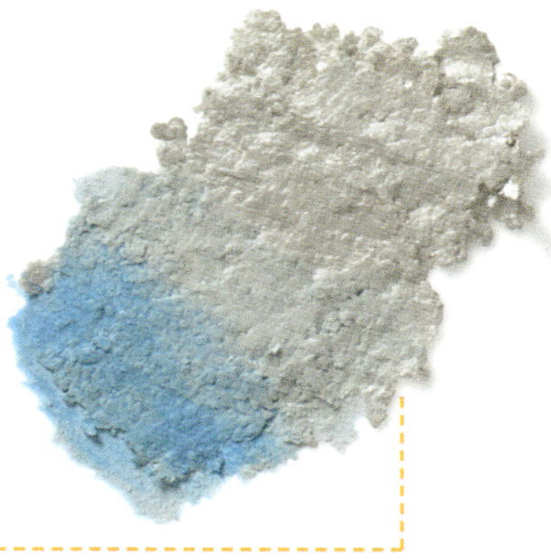

If you are going to use oil paint, let the textured mica base dry first *and then paint thin glazes over it to avoid obscuring its shininess completely.*

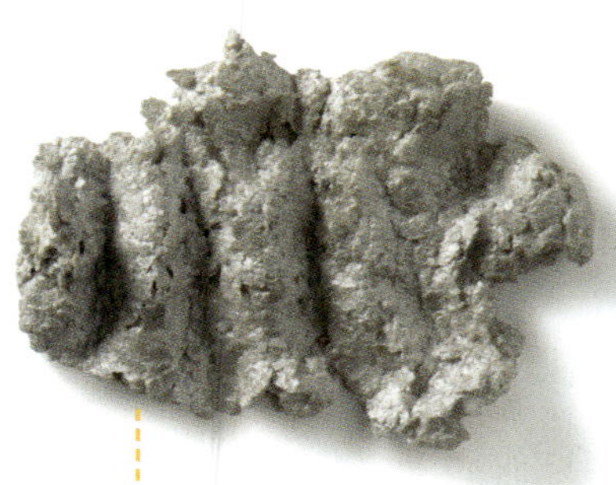

The small mica flakes add a satin sheen to the texture. *The shimmering reflections change according to the amount and direction of the light source.*

Shiny Textures

The addition of shiny fillers and glossy surfaces such as carborundum and mica creates artistic effects that would be impossible to obtain any other way. With this approach artists can achieve highly textured surfaces whose shininess varies according to the angle of the light source. Mica gel is made of a thick acrylic paste with natural mica which, upon drying, forms a texture of thick gray flakes and silvery reflections. Alternately, silicon carbide, a very dark and glossy material with the crystal structure of diamonds, can be added.

Volcanic Fillers

Black lava is often used by artists. It is not derived from the natural powdered lava, but from a thick paste of natural stone and black pigment. To create heavy relief, apply it in layers, letting each layer dry before the next one is applied. The drying time depends on the thickness of the layers and the weather, ranging between forty-five minutes and several hours. Pumice gel is an alternative to fine-textured gel. It is made of acrylic paste and pumice powder, which makes it lighter than other sand fillers of quartz or marble. Volcanic fillers are very abrasive and tend to wear out brushes very fast, especially if the painting is done very briskly.

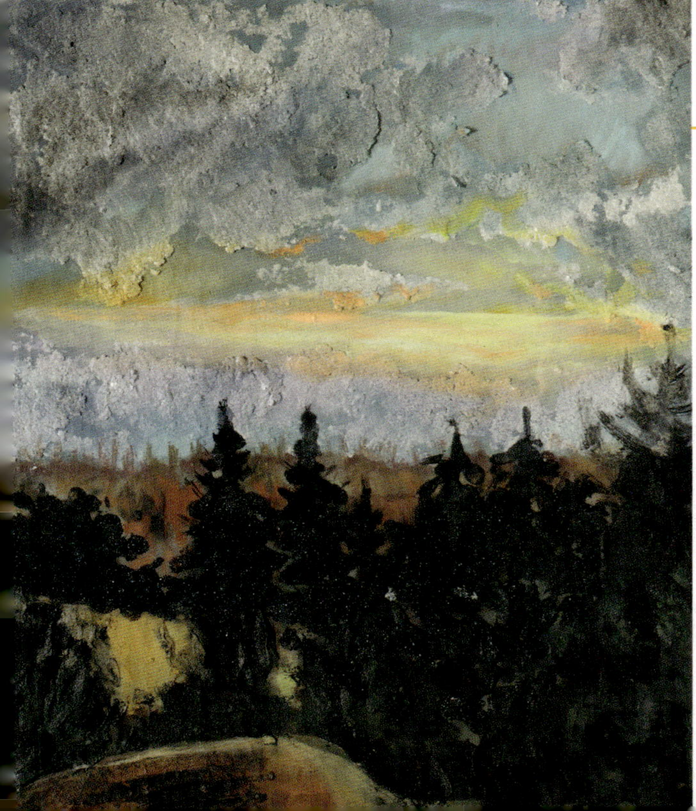

Sunset with thin oil glazes. *The textured base combines black lava and carborundum for the trees and mica gel for the clouds.*

IN THE STYLE OF...

Julian Schnabel (1951)

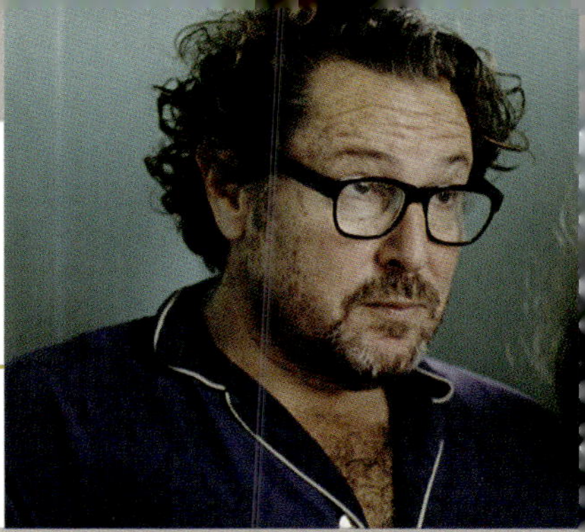

By the mid-eighties, Julian Schnabel had become an important figure in the Neo-Expressionist movement.

The Sea *(1981)*
This seascape forms part of the celebrated "plate paintings" made over broken ceramic plates. His work is known for its intense manifestation of personal style through daring textures. It often conveys great energy. His landscapes capture and hold on to the energy of the model, and they resemble abstractions more than natural scenes. This eclectic work references both the traditional treatment of landscape representation and a contemporary artistic approach.

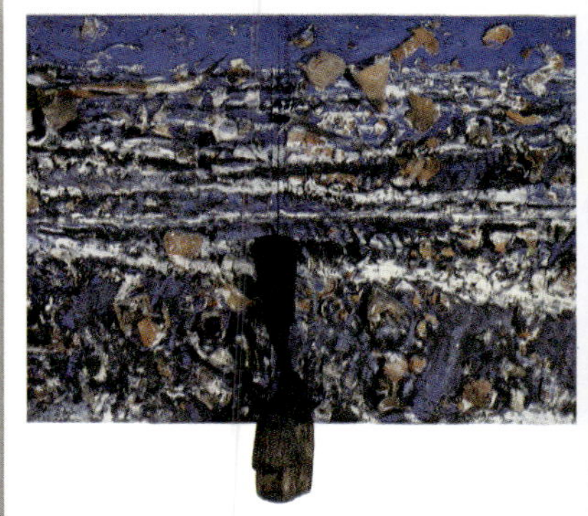

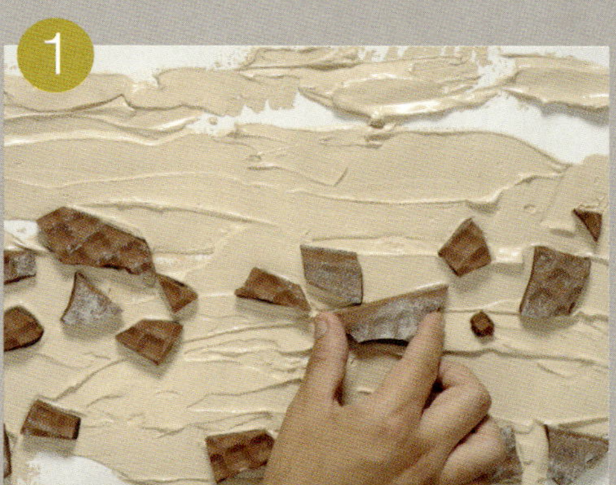

1. *We are going to try to reproduce the texture created by Schnabel in his painting. Glue pieces of ceramic tile over a surface of gesso. Make sure that they are securely adhered.*

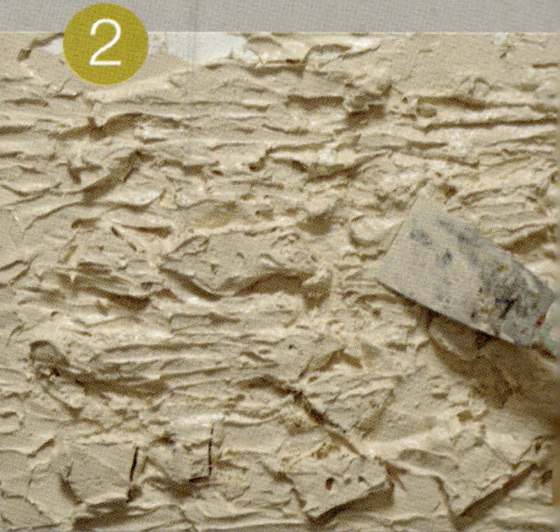

2. *When the gesso is dry, apply a second layer that will integrate the pieces of ceramic tile into the background, forming a pasty surface with an evenly striated tone.*

A New York artist and film director, Schnabel became known for his "plate paintings" made on pieces of broken plates and other ceramic dinnerware. From the outset of his career he showed a preference for larger formats based on collage and varied textures.

In the late 1970s, he began to use very unusual surfaces, like broken ceramic pieces, velvet, animal furs, and tar-coated heavy canvas. This particular characteristic of his work was in part influenced by the relevance of ceramic in the architecture of Antoni Gaudí.

THE INFLUENCE OF GAUDÍ

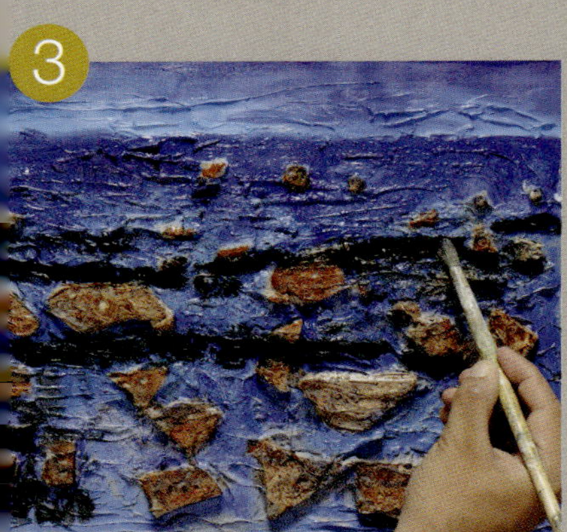

3. Wait one day for everything to dry completely. Paint the sea with cyan and ultramarine blue, avoiding the ceramic tile pieces, which will be painted with sienna. From this point on, you can begin using the rest of the colors.

4. Include white and black with a round bristle brush. Depositing the paint on the protruding areas without covering the background completely gives the finished painting a contemporary look.

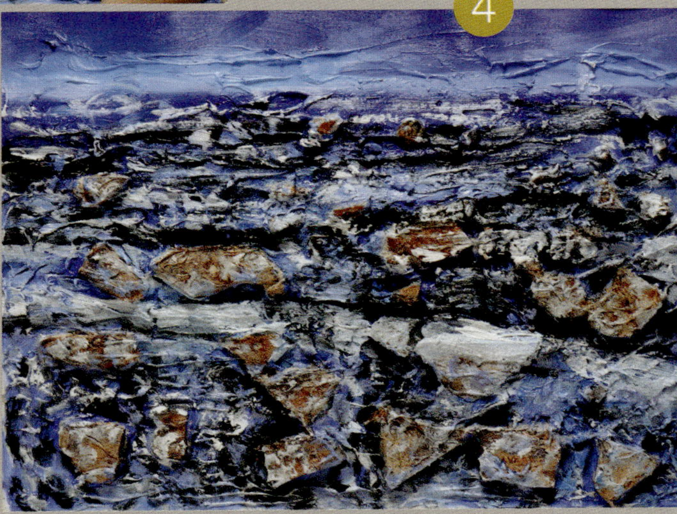

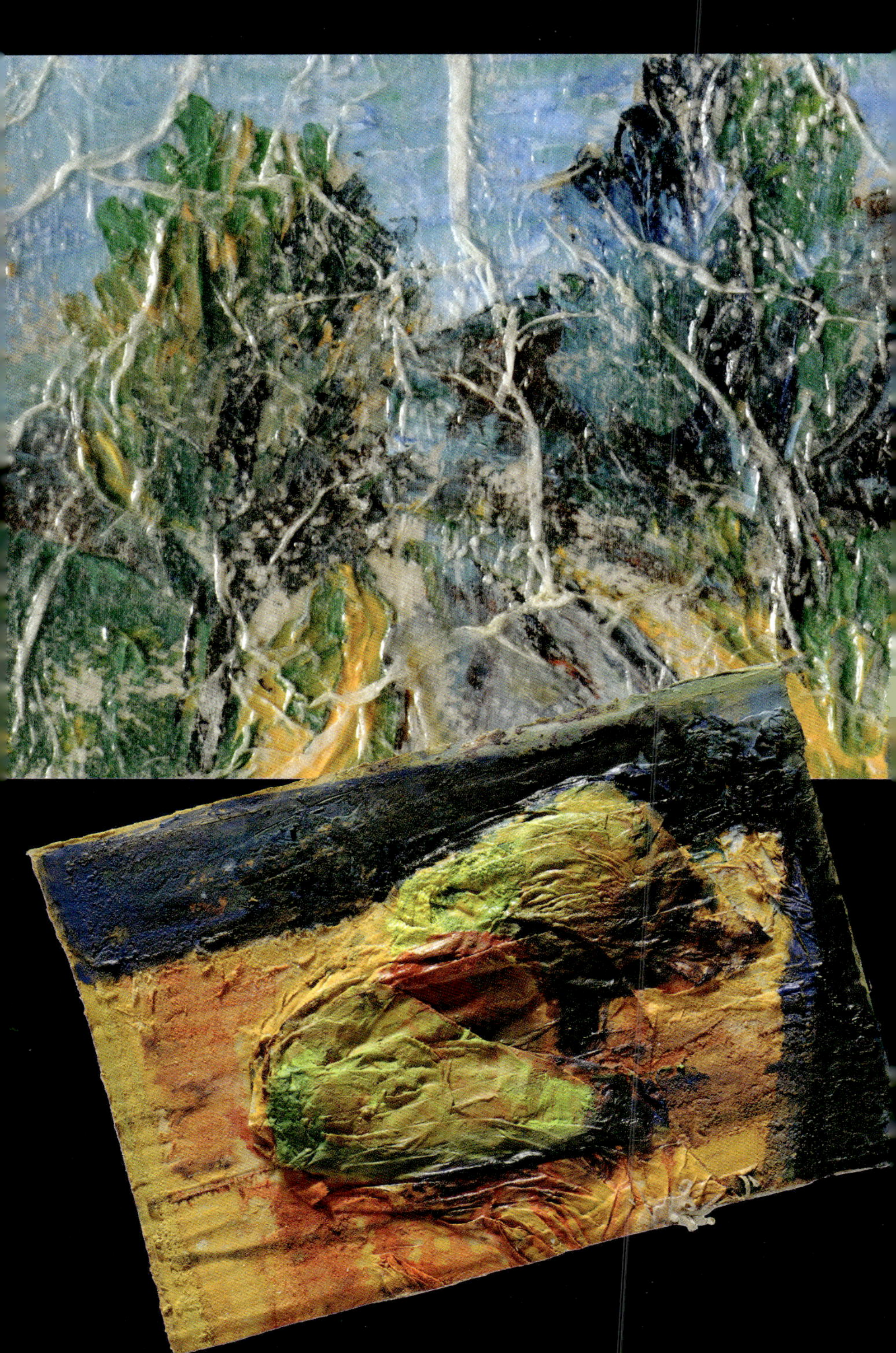

Painting over Textures

In this last section we explain the different ways that you can paint over textures, the color effects that can be achieved, and the challenges that can be expected. We will conclude with a few miscellaneous themes that, due to their distinctive nature, could not be included in the previous chapters. These all deal with textures created using materials not typically found in the world of painting.

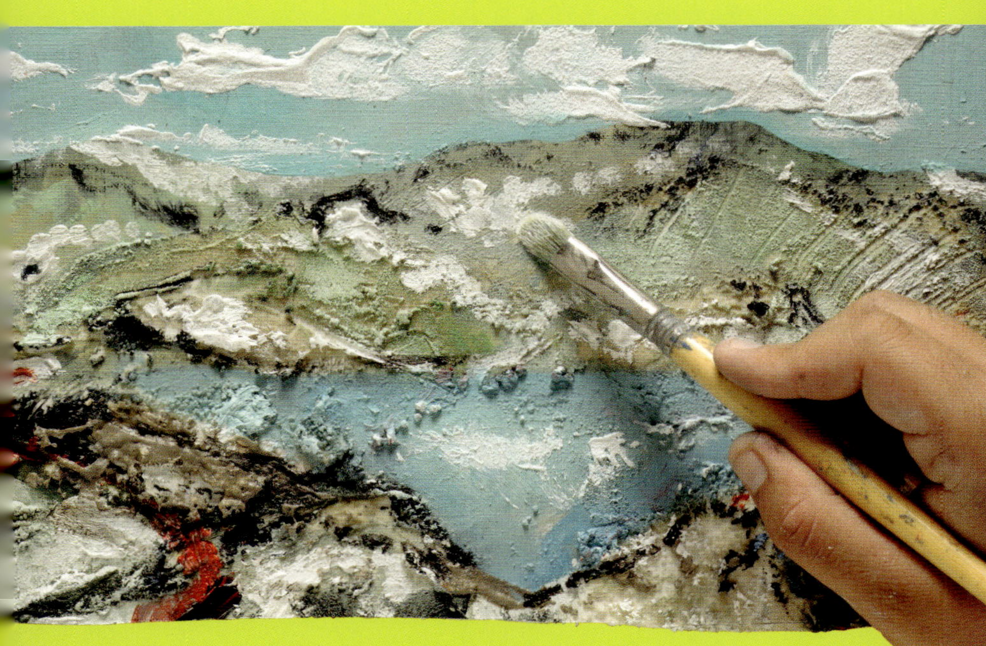

Dripping Paint

Acrylic paints can be dripped directly onto the support. This is easily done using a spout that comes with some cans of acrylic paint to control how much paint is dispensed. When drip painting, the artist must control the amount of paint with precision and must also handle it with ease. The drip itself makes a textured line whose thickness and volume depend on the size of the dispenser.

Painting with a spout is like drawing with a marker *whose line runs and has some relief.*

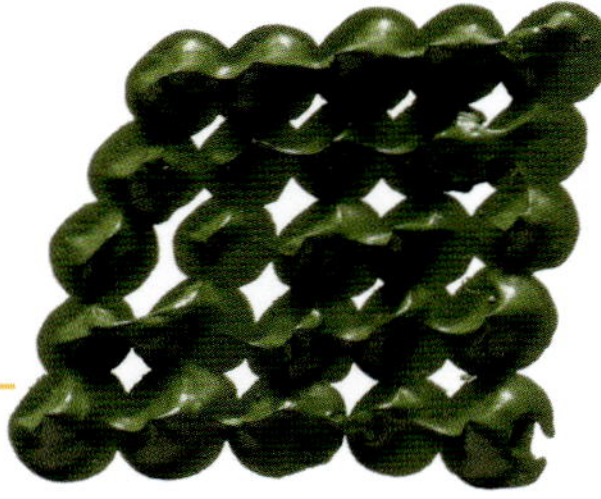

You do not have to paint in a straight line with drips; *you can also paint unusual textures with this technique.*

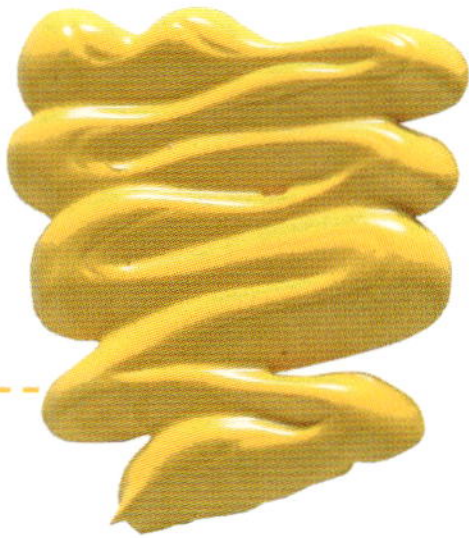

You can also drip paint with a tube, *but the line will be much thicker and you will use more paint.*

Here, we have applied dripped white paint over a support of the same color. *Then we have applied a blue wash, which highlights the relief of the dripped paint.*

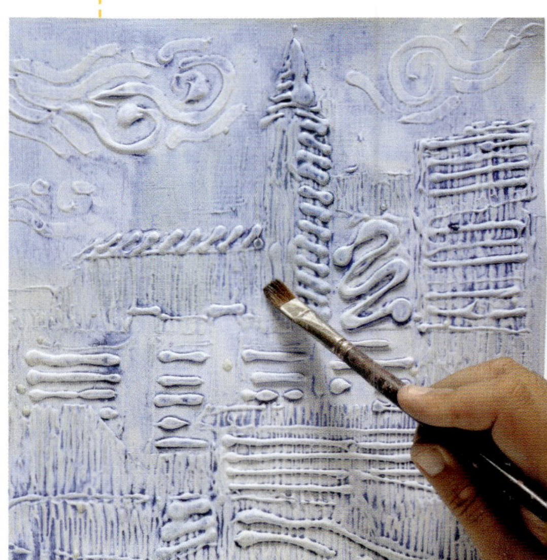

Cans with Dispensers

For this technique you will need a container with a dispenser or a glazing nozzle. If your containers come without these, you can buy small plastic bottles and fill them up with paint so you can paint directly with them. If they come with a spout, cut the tip with a craft knife, keeping in mind that the angle of the cut will determine the thickness of the line. We recommend that you start with a tiny cut and then cut more if you need a bigger opening. It is a good idea to work with a wide range of colors, because it is not easy to mix paint with this technique. Finally, you can even use paint straight from a tube, although sparingly, and only to make thick, heavy lines.

Mixing and Overlapping

There are two options when it comes to overlapping colors: wait for the first color to dry so the paints do not mix together, or mix the colors wet on wet. With this latter approach the colors may look somewhat cloudy if the paint is not applied carefully. You can also build up the surface relief with drips, wait until they dry and then paint over with glazes again to emphasize the volume even more.

Because of the lengthy drying time of oil paints, *it is better to use acrylics for dripping because they dry in only a few hours and you will be able to add new paint over the already dry surface.*

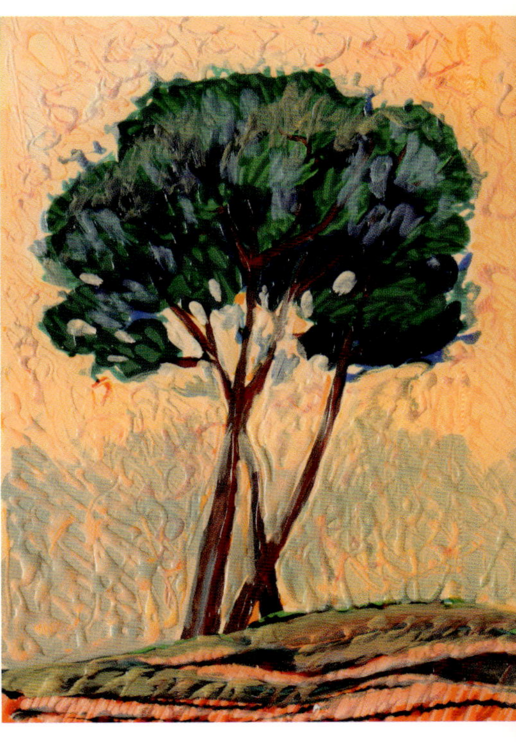

There are small plastic tubes available *that can be refilled with different color paints that already come with a spout or a nozzle, ready for painting.*

THE SUBJECT

Washes over Textures

When the surface relief of a painting that has been created with gesso or modeling paste turns white after drying, it can be painted over with a thin layer of diluted paint. This creates an interesting combination between the paint and the texture, in such a way that it is hard to know where one begins and the other ends.

Oil paint looks like a glaze, *where the luminosity of the color does not come from the lightness of the color mixture but rather from the white color of the support.*

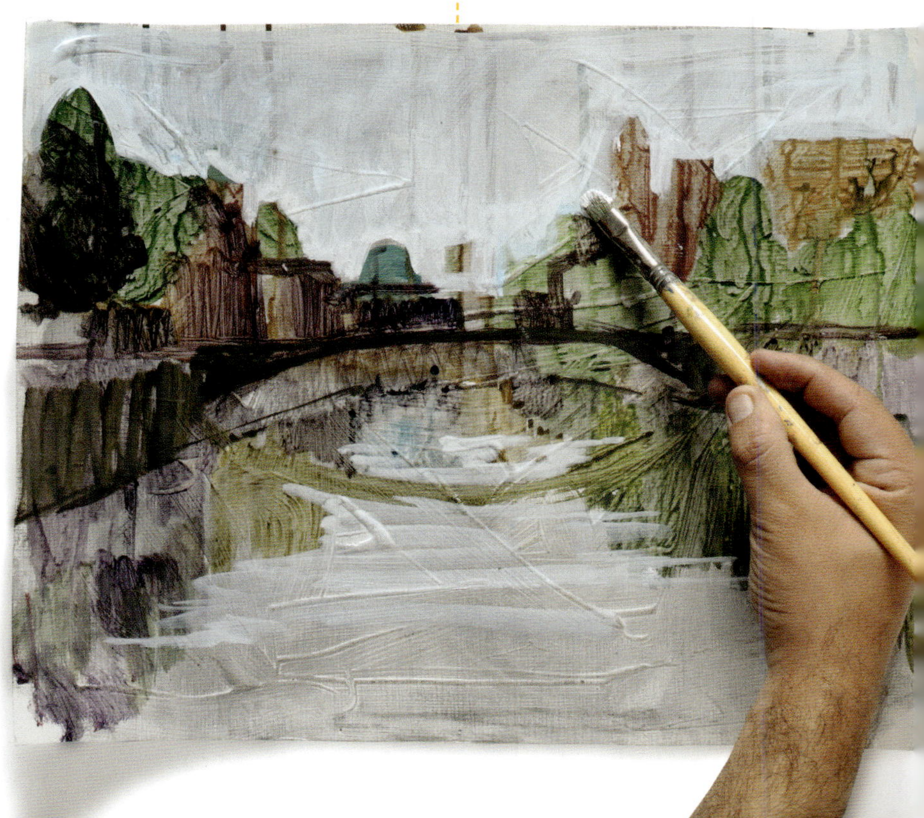

Preparing the Surface

Before applying the paint, the surface must be primed with modeling paste or gesso. Spread it with a spatula and make any marks or texture that you like. The surface should not be too smooth; it should have texture, like the surface of the moon or tree bark. When the gesso is dry, paint over it with very diluted glazes. The diluted color is deposited into the grooves giving the surface a three-dimensional appearance. Once the acrylic paint dries, it will look like the impasto was created with the color of the glaze.

Painting with Glazes

To paint with glazes we recommend that you use acrylics instead of oil paints because they dry faster. This does not mean that you cannot do glazing with oil paints, but you will have to wait three or four days between layers. With acrylics, on the other hand, after applying one layer over the white gesso you need wait only about half an hour before applying a second one. You will need to wait the same length of time, more or less, for the third layer. When the layers dry out you will notice how each one changes the way the final color looks. This effect will be more obvious in the lower areas where the paint tends to accumulate.

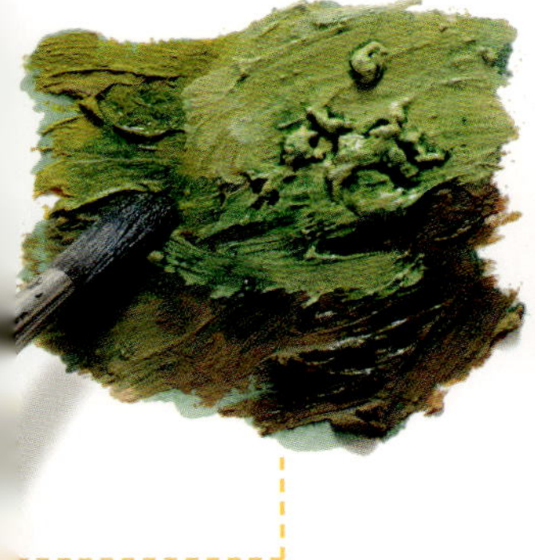

Diluted paint is deposited in the crevices of the gesso texture that is already dry. *If you layer various glazes, the resulting color will be surprising.*

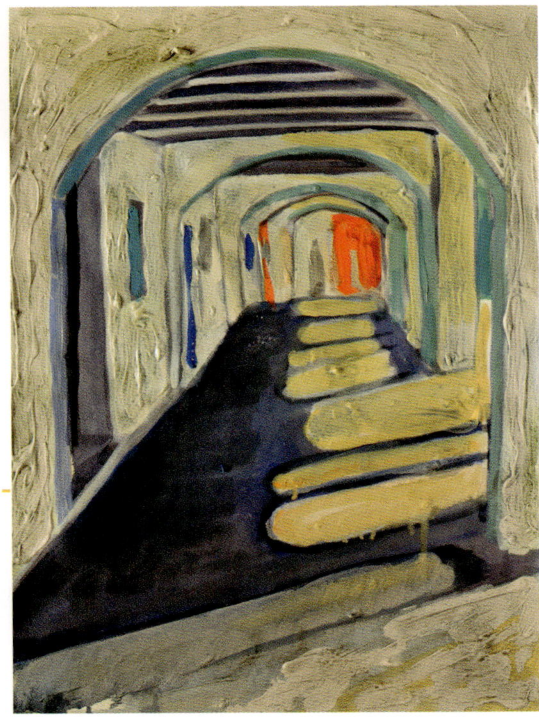

Textured areas can be combined with smooth areas. *We have applied texture with gesso on the walls and arches to create striations and relief effects when the color glazes are applied.*

LET'S EXPERIMENT

Glazes with Acrylics

In this view of a lake the foreground is covered with vegetation and the background is dominated by shades of blue.

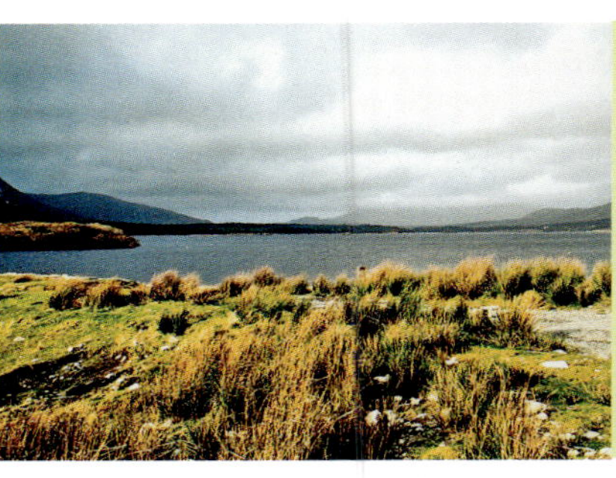

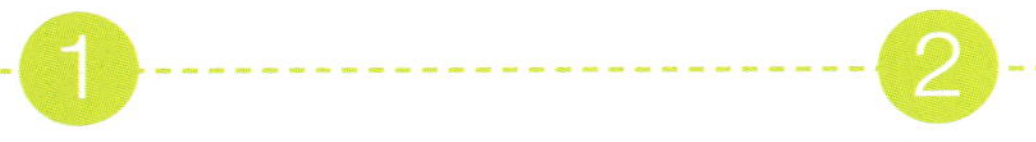

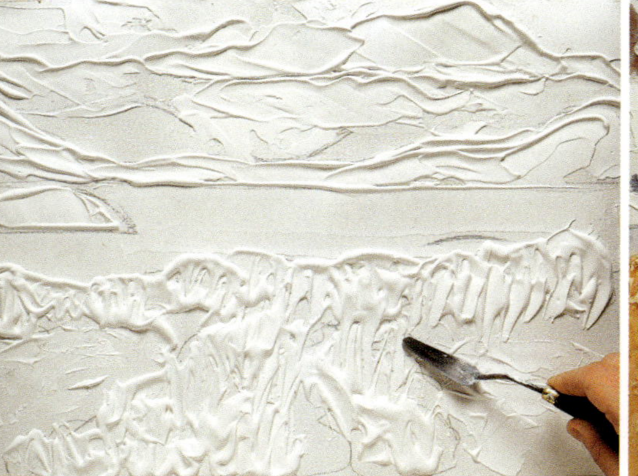

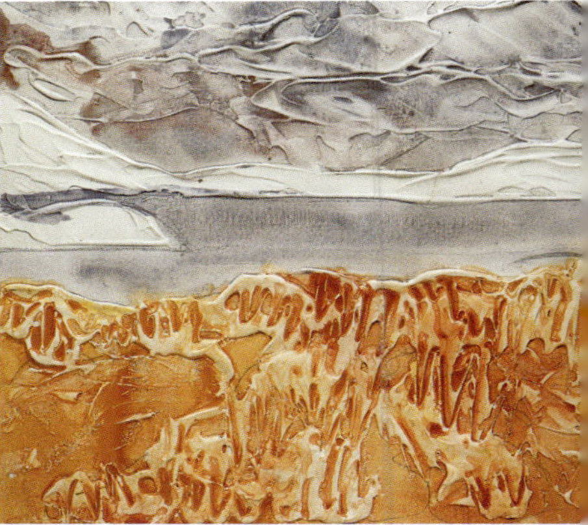

1. *Using a medium spatula, apply the gesso to form the main features of the landscape, as if it were a bas-relief.*

2. *When the gesso is dry cover each area with a first layer of very diluted acrylic paint. The color will be darker in the crevices while it will appear lighter on the raised areas.*

3. *When the previous washes have dried out, apply new glazes, less extensively this time, paying attention to the particular color of each area.*

4. *Gabriel Martín finishes the exercise with two or three different glazes. The vegetation requires more layering while he uses a smaller amount of paint for the sky and the lake.*

When you apply glazes with acrylic paint over a surface textured with gesso, the diluted paint tends to puddle in the crevices and cracks, making the raised areas lighter than the receding ones.

Here we will explain this effect briefly with a very simple exercise. It can be executed in just a few minutes if the gesso surface is completely dry and hard.

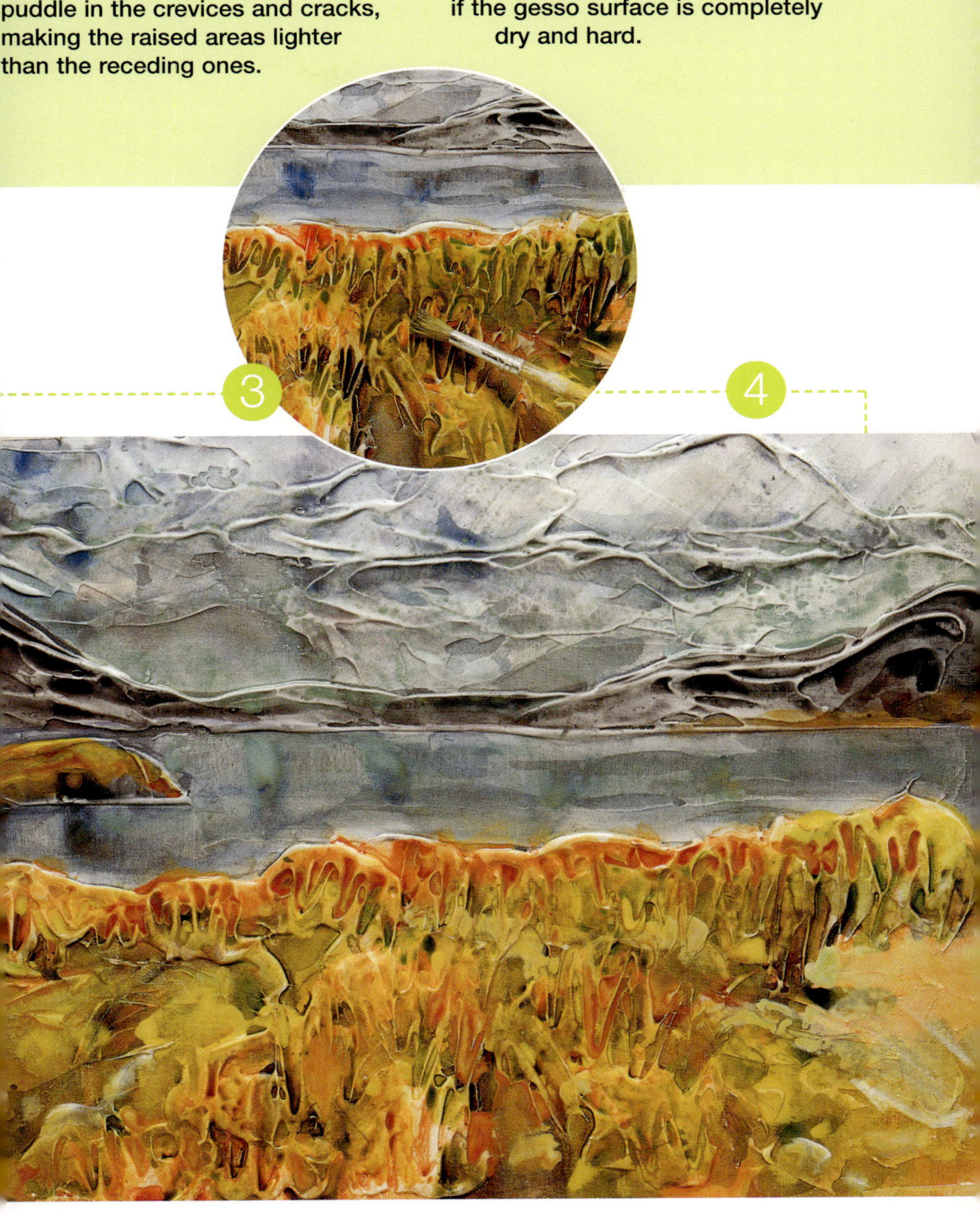

THE SUBJECT

Using Newsprint for Volume

This time, we will use crumpled newspapers to create very high relief and protruding volume. This technique was developed in the spirit of recycling and of using everyday materials, by the followers of *Arte Povera*. (In Italian this means "poor art."). The artistic movement became popular during the latter part of the seventies and its creators used inexpensive, easy to find, and/or throw-away materials.

A newspaper is considered a disposable item *that has neither material nor artistic value. It does not normally evoke beautiful or exquisite thoughts.*

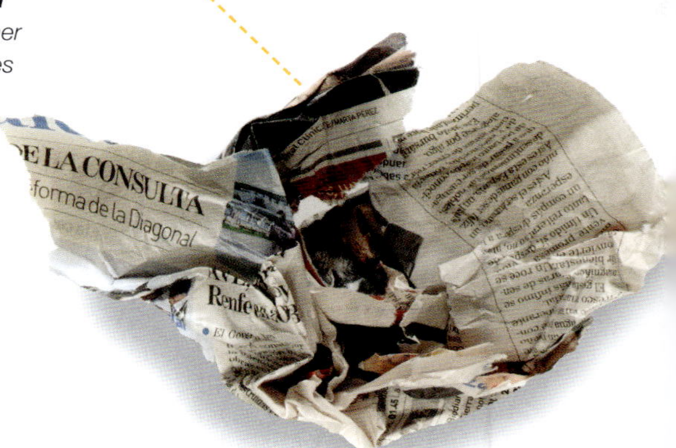

On a surface treated with gesso it is easier to paint with oils. *The use of newspapers shows the artist's focus on everyday objects—items that don't normally inspire artistic expression.*

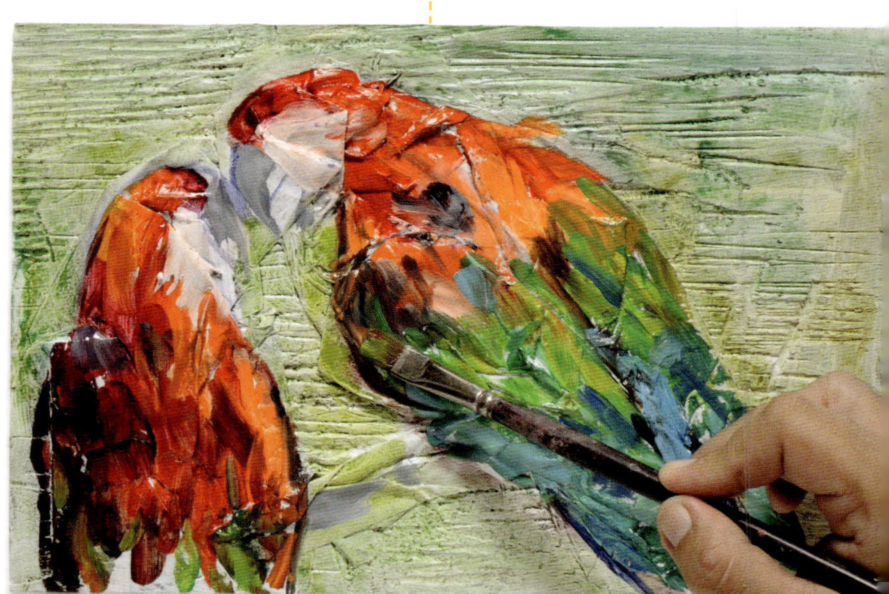

The Value of Paper

Newspapers are thrown away, do not have any value, and can be easily obtained. When you soak them with white glue they can create strong bas-relief effects on the surface of a painting. The goal is to bring out and to enhance the natural volume and shape of an object by manipulating the material. The use of crumpled newspapers also represents a clear rejection of the increasing abuse of the chemical additives found in mediums and gels.

Crumple and Glue

To prepare the newspaper relief, first take a few pages and crumple them to form balls. Then cover the support with generous amounts of glue and press the paper balls onto it. The paper should be arranged according to your planned design, following the idea of the elements that you wish to represent. Press the crumpled paper with a brush soaked in white glue; wait a few minutes until it dries. Then, cover it with a thin layer of white gesso; this way the textured surface will provide a base ready to be painted.

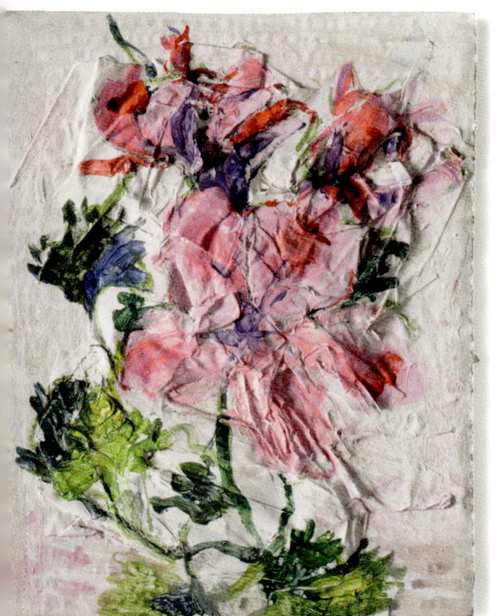

The newspapers can be used to represent everyday subjects, *like these flowers, with unrefined and undefined textures, but charged with a whimsical spirit.*

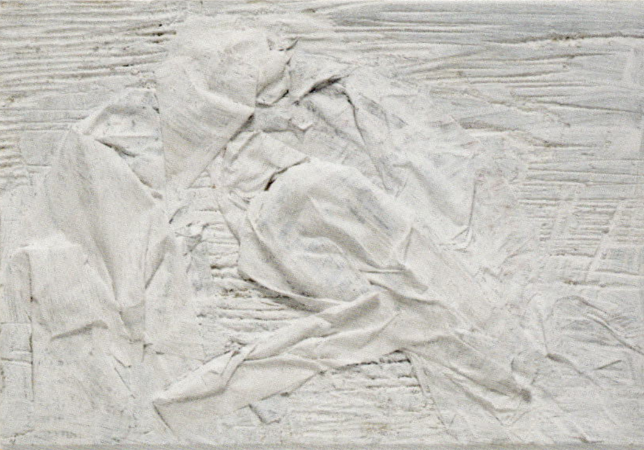

Add the crumpled paper to a surface covered with glue. *Once it dries, cover it with a thin layer of gesso. The shape of the paper should represent the form of the model.*

THE SUBJECT

Varnish and Wrinkles

In this exercise we are going to make a brief foray into drawing. For this, we are going to experiment with the use of varnish on paper to create interesting glazes, relief, and textured effects. We are also going to explain how to create a crackled effect, which, in addition to acting as a glaze, can add interest to a drawing, giving it a very contemporary finish.

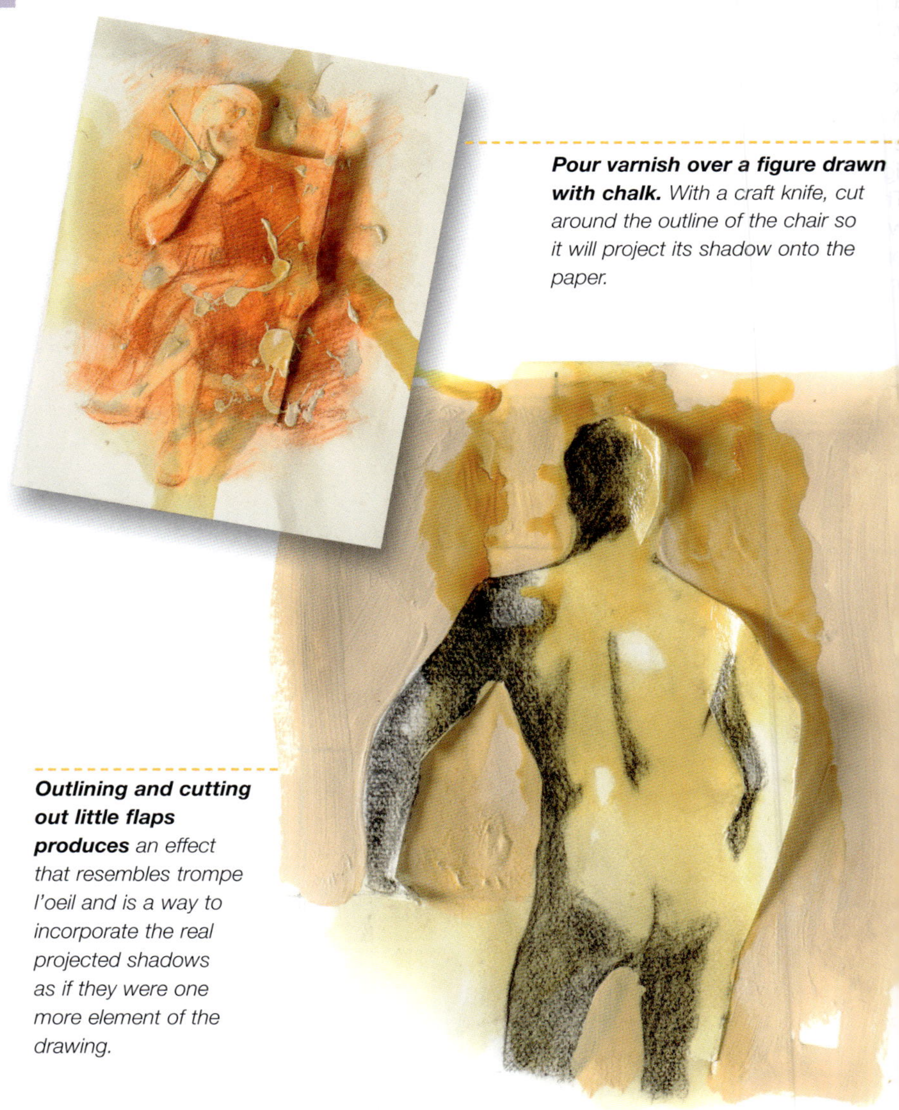

Pour varnish over a figure drawn with chalk. *With a craft knife, cut around the outline of the chair so it will project its shadow onto the paper.*

Outlining and cutting out little flaps produces *an effect that resembles trompe l'oeil and is a way to incorporate the real projected shadows as if they were one more element of the drawing.*

Cutouts and Folds

To create a contemporary representation of any drawn figure, you can pour aging varnish over the paper. It is browner in tone than the finishing varnish used for paintings. The varnish does not conceal the drawing, but instead it forms a soft brown glaze that hardens the paper. You must wait a day for it to dry completely. Then, with a very sharp craft knife cut out a few areas of the figures. Lift the cutouts to make them stand out as if they were flaps, to create a *trompe l'oeil* effect—the illusion is that part of the figure is coming towards the viewer. These flaps, when lit from the side with strong lighting, project a shadow on the drawing that produces a very interesting effect.

Crackled Surfaces

Over a drawing done with charcoal, chalk, or a similar medium, you can spread a thin layer of paper kitchen towel to create a crackled glaze effect. (Toilet paper also works—the thinner the sheet of paper, the better.) First, separate the various layers that form the sheet of paper and adhere one with a fast-drying varnish. The paper will act as a whitish glaze that will look crackled all over due to the effect of the varnish. This way the drawing will have an unusual finish.

The aging or crackling varnishes are the most effective finishes in these cases. *They dry fast and produce a very characteristic brown color.*

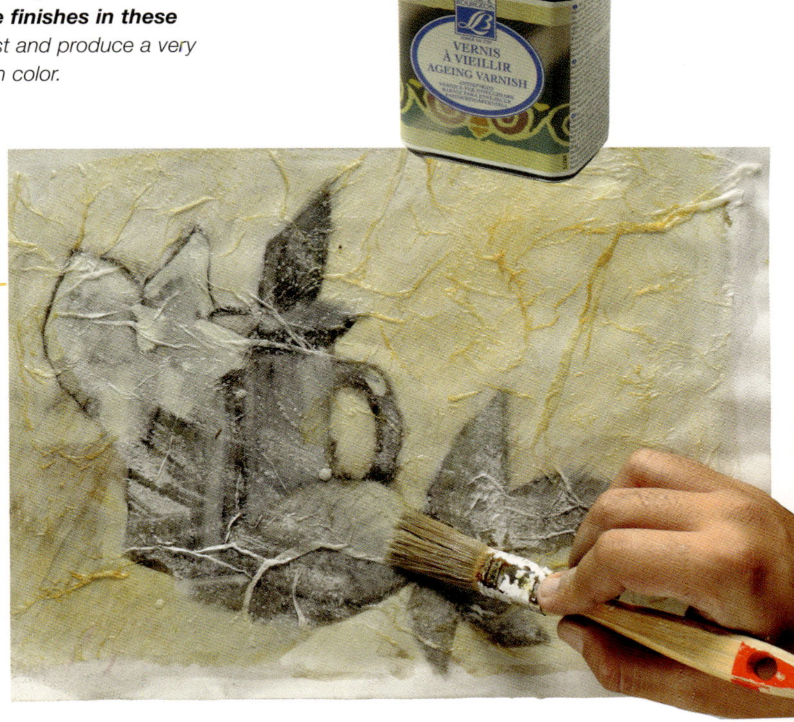

Lay a thin sheet of paper towel over the drawing done with charcoal or wash. Secure it to the base with varnish. *This will produce a crackled effect that totally changes the look of the drawing.*

THE SUBJECT

Pure Abstraction

Abstract painting is probably the one approach that allows the artist to mix a wide variety of textures on a single support, combining the most diverse, even contradictory, media. This approach does not necessarily result in a finished painting, but can also be used as an archive of interesting test samples of uncommon textures and materials.

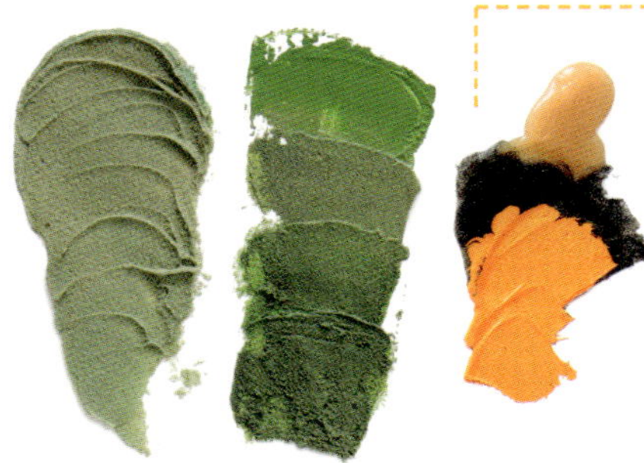

Do not be afraid of mixing materials that look different. *Experimentation is the way to discover new textures.*

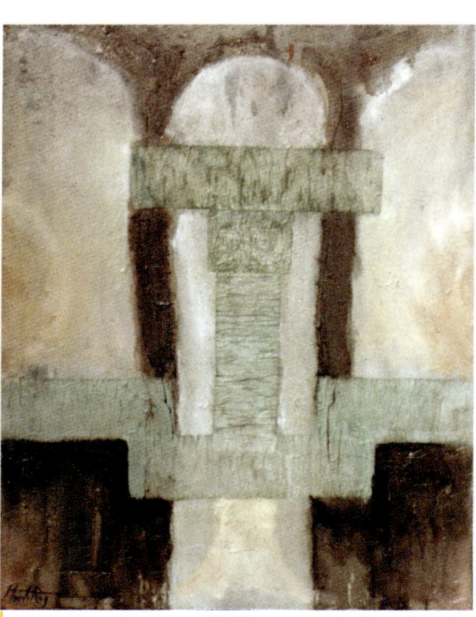

Abstract forms created with toilet tissue glued over a background of latex and marble dust. *When it dried out, it was completely covered with oil glazes.*

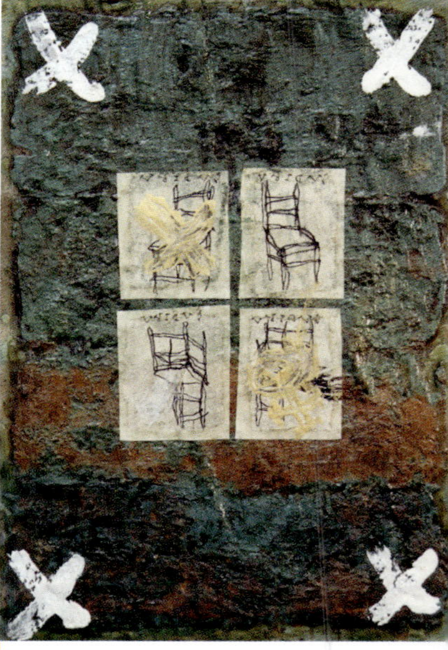

The support is a thin sheet of bronze *that has been treated with nitric acid diluted with water to create a rusted and corroded effect. A few months later, when the reaction is complete, it is painted over with varnish.*

A Liberating Experience

If you are not an enthusiast of abstract painting, you should think of these exercises as a liberating experience, as an opportunity to experiment with the various possibilities afforded by the combinations of different materials. Experimentation is needed to see how they will work together, how different materials can be combined, as well as to evaluate the required drying times. In order to proceed effectively, have small pieces of cardboard handy for combining textures, making color notes, and completing small studies about any subject matter.

The Tactile Quality

In abstract paintings with heavy texture, the tactile quality of the materials becomes more relevant than the colors. This does not mean that the artist should totally disregard color, but texture should become the focal point. If possible, the artist should try to avoid repetitive patterns and alternate different types of textures to create a rhythm, enhancing the tactile quality of the painting and achieving a more pronounced effect.

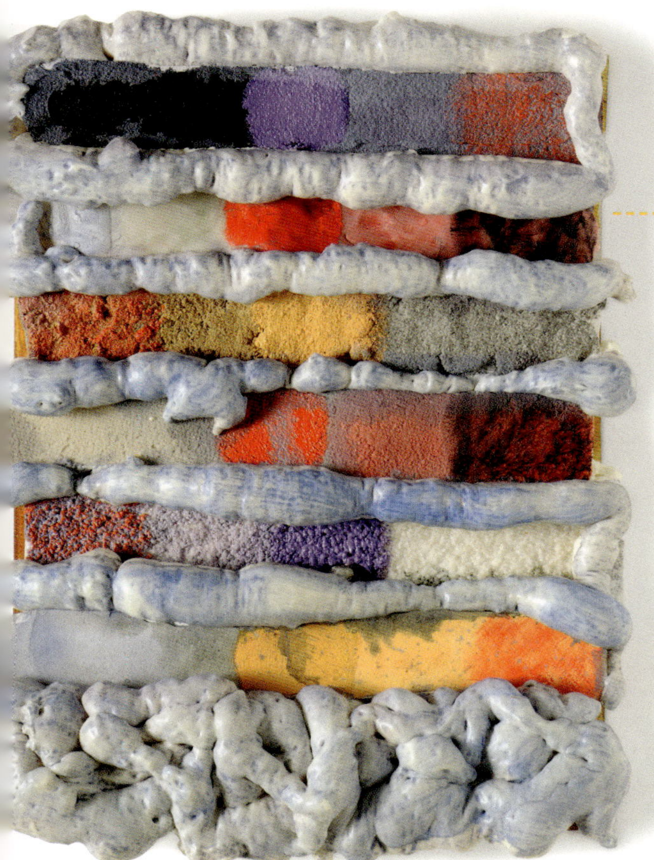

Different textures and colors alternate *forming the rhythmic effect of this pattern made of horizontal bands painted with reddish, blue, and violet tones.*

THE SUBJECT

Volume with Wax

Wax is not commonly used by artists because it is difficult and awkward to manipulate; however, this oily substance added to oils increases its volume and changes its consistency. It is a good alternative to oleopasto. There are two basic ways of working with it: warm and in gel form.

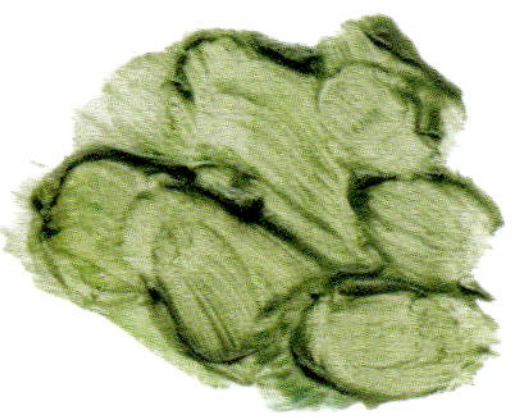

If you mix large quantities of wax with oil paint *the resulting effects will be creamy and transparent.*

Wax enhances the color *of the oil paint, but it also takes away its glossiness.*

Oil paints mixed with wax *can be applied either with a brush or with a spatula.*

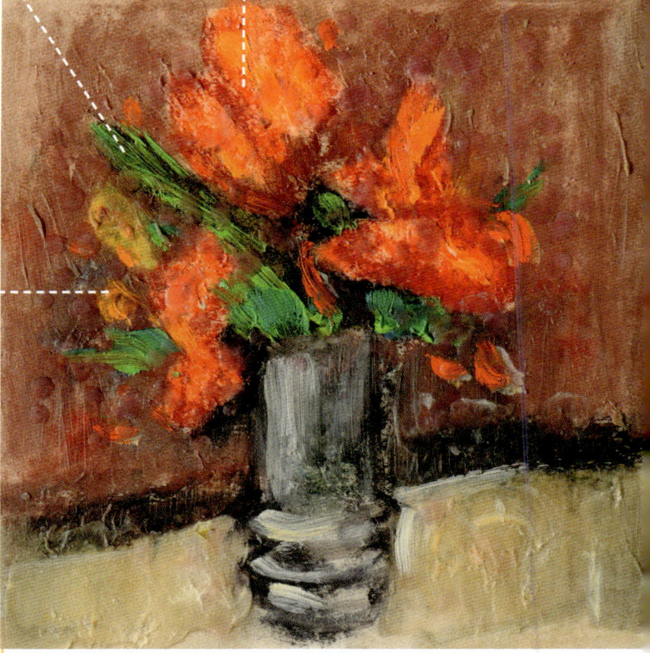

A vase with flowers painted with wax and oils. *Each oil color has been mixed beforehand on the palette with wax gel. This gives the surface a completely creamy appearance.*

Encaustic Paint

This is the name given to painting with oils and wax. The most common way of working with encaustics is to place them on a metal palette mounted on four drinking glasses to keep it elevated above the table. Two candles are placed underneath to keep the wax hot.

Melt a piece of white wax in a double boiler beforehand. With a metal spoon, deposit the melted wax on the metal palette and mix it with the oil paint. Pick up the mixture with the brush and paint over the support. Move the brush briskly since you will only have a few seconds before the mixture of paint and wax hardens the bristles, which upon making contact with the hot surface of the palette will soften again. The result is a painting where the colors bunch together, forming lumps and waxy effects with a characteristic satin finish.

Wax with Gel

Recently, a gel wax has become available that does not require the use of a hot palette. It has the consistency of lard or shoe polish cream and it has a very strong odor. It is very creamy and can be mixed with oils while cold. Like paint, it can be dissolved with turpentine and the final result is very similar to the one obtained with hot wax but without the inconvenience. It has a downside which is its long drying time. It can take one or two months to dry if the thickness of the impasto is greater than three-sixteenths of an inch (5 mm).

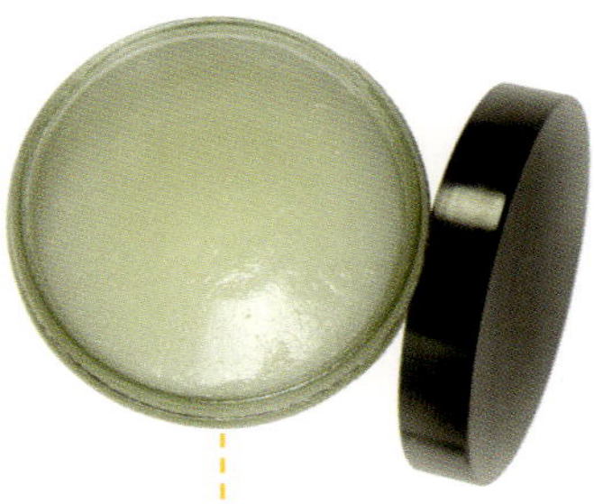

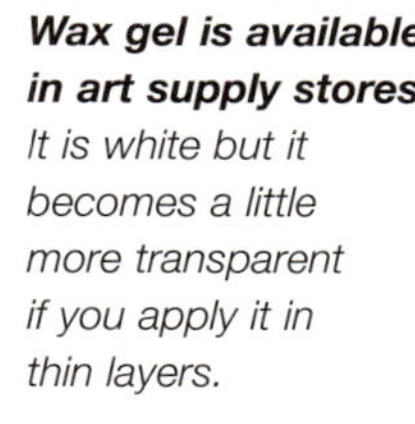

Wax gel is available in art supply stores. *It is white but it becomes a little more transparent if you apply it in thin layers.*

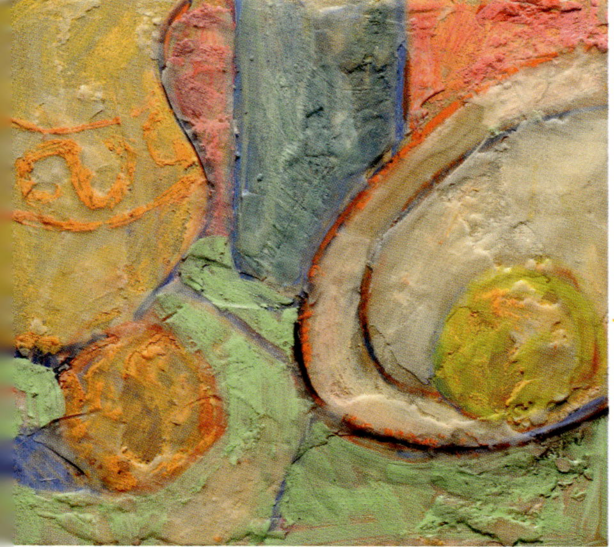

A colorist still life with a mixture of oil and hot wax. *The texture of the wax combines the transparency and the impasto.*

The Plasticity of Texture

After reviewing a great many materials that can be incorporated into a painting to create deep relief effects, it is time for hands-on experimentation and for working some of them on the support with conviction. Be inspired by the plasticity of the texture; maximize the possibilities of each material to obtain interesting compositions of great artistic value.

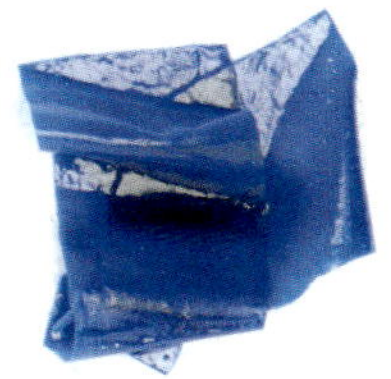

Thin pieces of latex form *very curvy and rounded wrinkles. Glue the latex to the support with white glue.*

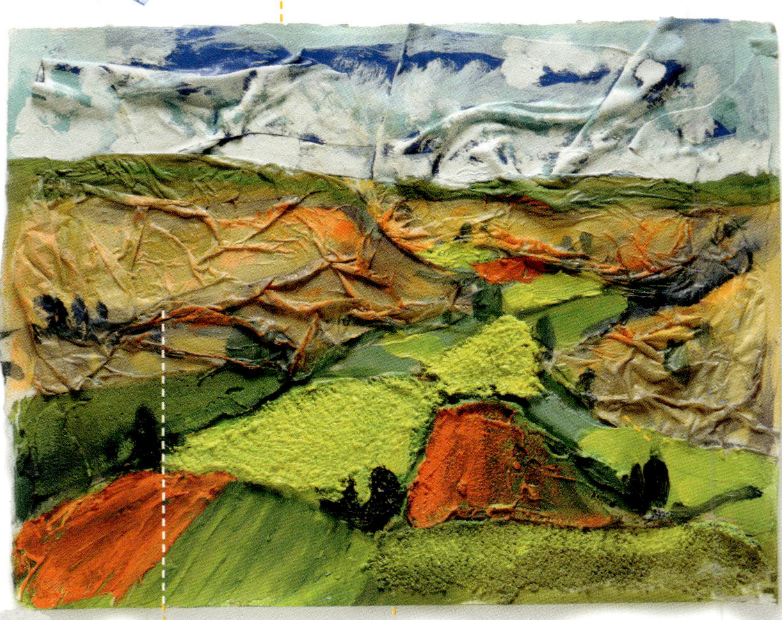

A white plastic bag *can be an excellent alternative to wrinkled paper.*

Be daring and use all kinds of materials on the painting, *no matter how unusual they may be. Each material has its own physical characteristics and quality, which adds variety to the painting. This landscape has been created with pieces of latex, a plastic bag, and a fine and medium textured gel.*

Texture over Texture

Once you have experimented with a variety of materials, you should begin to think of ways to combine them creatively on the canvas, as if it were a collage. The physical characteristics of each material should mimic the surface of the real model that you wish to represent. The textures can be overlapped or juxtaposed as if they were painted surfaces, the difference being that in this instance you are not only dealing with color but also with various features like folds and lumps in the materials you choose to incorporate.

Changing Planes

Plan two simple landscapes using various materials or modeling paste that you may have available. First, do a simple pencil sketch of the model that you want to paint. Glue on the painting the materials that you have chosen to use to create an interesting relief representation of the model. The materials should have certain affinity with the real texture of the model. Wait a day for the glue to dry completely. If you plan to paint with oils you can begin now; on the other hand, if you are using acrylics you will need to cover the entire textured surface with a layer of white gesso so the paint will adhere properly.

Prepare the texture of the ground with thin noodles and a few twigs to represent the tree trunks. *Gesso is used in certain areas of the painting to minimize the hardness of the texture.*

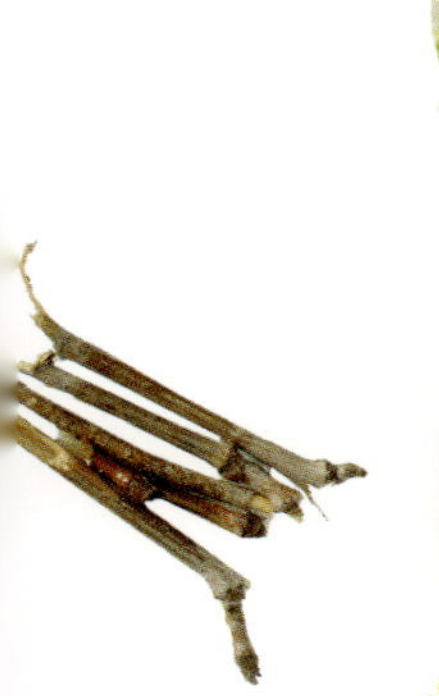

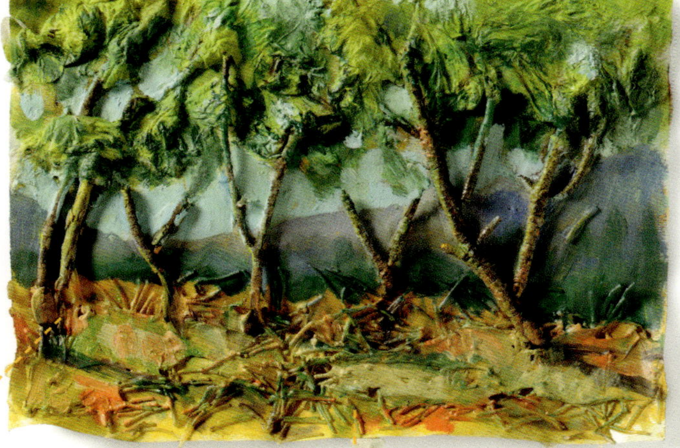

The use of small twigs creates a lot of texture *in the central part of the composition. The branches can be covered with a touch of gesso so they do not look so dark.*

Once the thin noodles have been glued on, *it is a good idea to apply another layer of glue to secure them to the surface and prevent them from falling off while painting.*

THE SUBJECT

A Landscape with Organic Materials

The use of more ephemeral, organic materials, taken from nature, is in some way a return to primitive art. It represents another point of departure from western art theory, which states that painting should be done on valuable materials, capable of standing the test of time, in parallel with the idea of immortality. Organic materials are a good alternative to the seriousness of reflective painting.

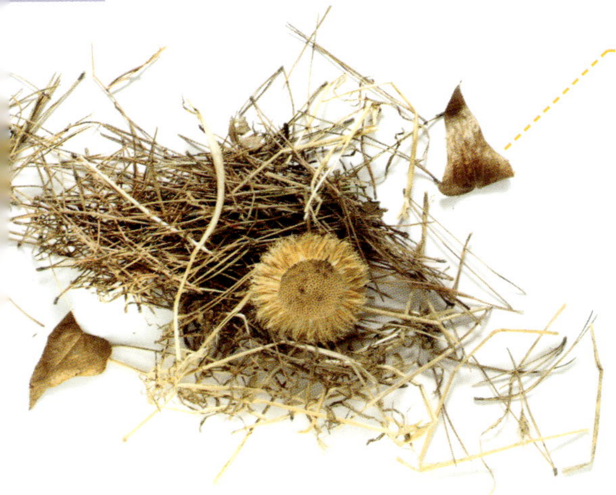

Any organic material that can be collected in the forest or in the fields can be incorporated into the canvas. *It should be dry material. Never use tender shoots or flowers, unless they have been dried.*

Adhere the straw and branches to the support with a large amount of white glue *to make sure they are secure. Before painting, you can cove them with a light layer of gesso.*

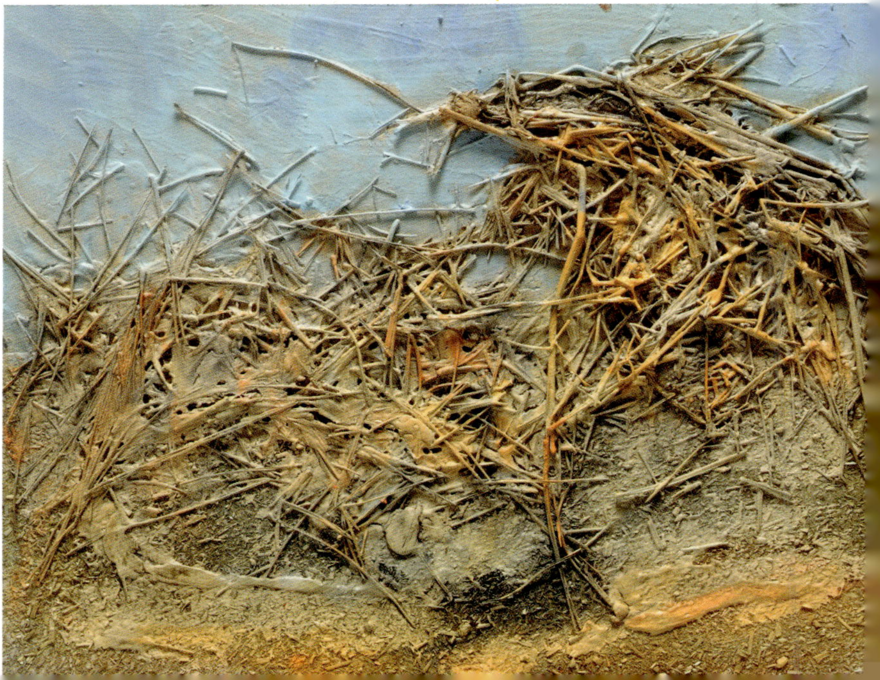

Straw and Foliage

Art may express the ephemeral quality of human life by way of durable materials, but there is no reason to rule out the use of fragile materials, such as flowers, straw, or branches, to complement the transitory character of our existence. To that end, one can cover a painting with dense textures of foliage and straw—materials associated more with forests than with a canvas. Be careful and use organic materials that are completely dry. Young shoots or green leaves are not suitable because they rot and turn black, which can ruin the effect of the painting.

Indigenous Art

In the art of primitive cultures, the importance of materials was very different from our current conventional thinking. Straw and branches were considered to be nobler than a valuable imported piece of fabric. The use of ephemeral materials may seem a lesser painting method; however, the aesthetic of using organic elements and the return to nature and ancestral values have become new trends in painting, ones which broaden our concept of what "art" is. In a painting, an artist can very effectively combine areas of oil or acrylic paint with areas of texture created with organic elements. These natural materials are, in fact, often used to represent vegetation itself.

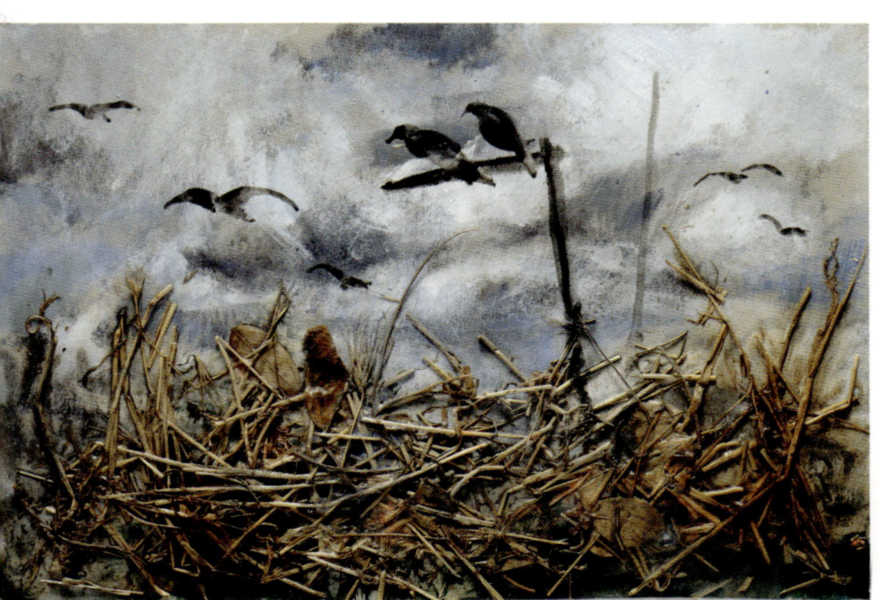

A painting finished with organic materials. *Areas painted exclusively with oils are combined with others treated with texture. The straw in the background is used to represent a real element of the landscape, making the work more realistic.*

THE SUBJECT

Using Objects in Collage

The technique of adding fillers can make a painting look very busy; however, it is possible to create a work of great simplicity and beauty by incorporating small fragments of objects. The three-dimensionality of these types of paintings is very pronounced and the results can be very gratifying. They give us the opportunity to appreciate the creative potential of each unique material employed.

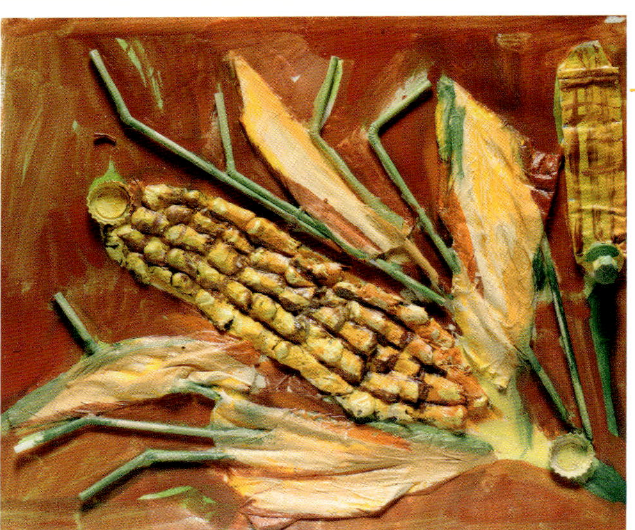

Almost anything can be used to create relief: *pieces of straw or stems, bottle caps, cigarette butts, even a used tube of oil paint. The idea is to combine them gracefully to create a pleasing effect.*

The materials should be adapted and manipulated as needed. *The term trencadis, coined by the architect Gaudí, defines a technique consisting of breaking up tiles to make shards. These can then be incorporated into the painting.*

Not everything is appropriate. *For obvious reasons, sharp pieces of glass should not be used, but glass with rounded edges, like the ones often found on beaches, are fine.*

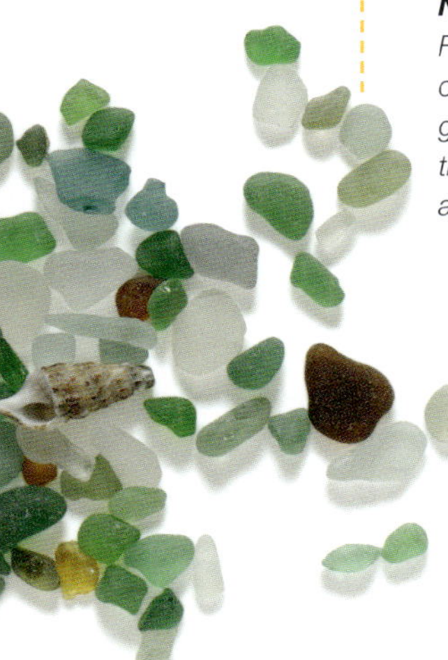

Anything Goes

Crumpled paper, aluminum foil, tile shards, leaves, stones, cork, plastic objects, or distressed wood can all be adhered to the support with glue. At this primary step, details are not important; what matters is the precise and careful distribution of the elements. Wait at least one day for the pieces to adhere properly. Before painting, cover all the glued objects with a layer of gesso. In addition to smoothing the surface, gesso provides a porous base that ensures proper adhesion of the oil or acrylic paint. This white primer also prevents the paint from being affected by the original color of the objects.

Optimum Adherence

There are several excellent adhesives that become transparent once dry, such as latex, white glue, and acrylic gel. Consequently, they are ideal for sticking collage materials to the support ad encrusting them in a thick layer of fresh paint or over modeling paste. When objects are adhered, it is important to keep the support flat until the adhesive is dry. On an upright support the wet paste would start sliding and dragging with it the collage materials.

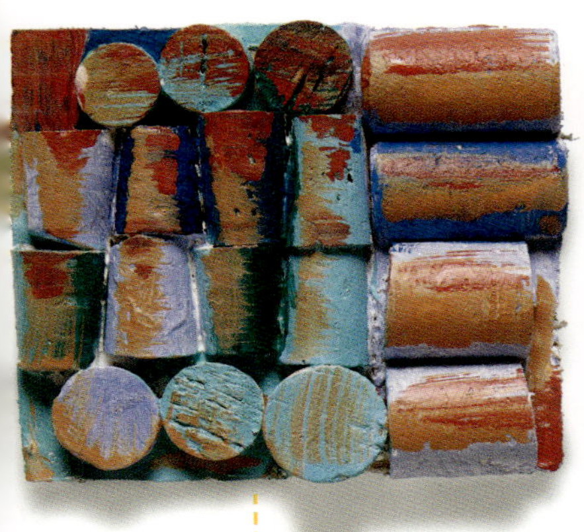

You can create interesting geometric reliefs with cut-up corks. *Furthermore, the texture of this material takes oil and acrylic paint very well.*

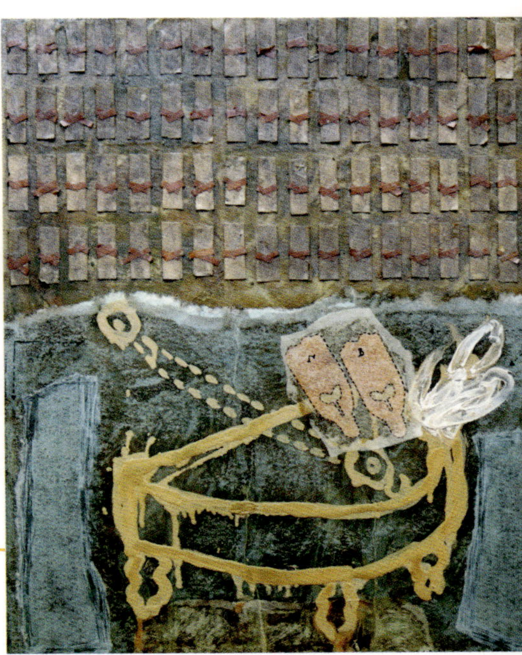

Small pieces of rolled leather have been incorporated on the upper part of the painting. *This creates a rhythmic and repetitive three-dimensional effect—a nice contrast to the wide brushstrokes at the bottom.*

Relief with Foam

Polyurethane foam is a very versatile material. Depending on the additives and the manufacturing process used, it can be used to create very unusual reliefs, which give a painting a very unusual and original look. This solid, uniform, and durable product, which is light and can be easily applied, has a cellular structure that is suitable for use as a relief paste.

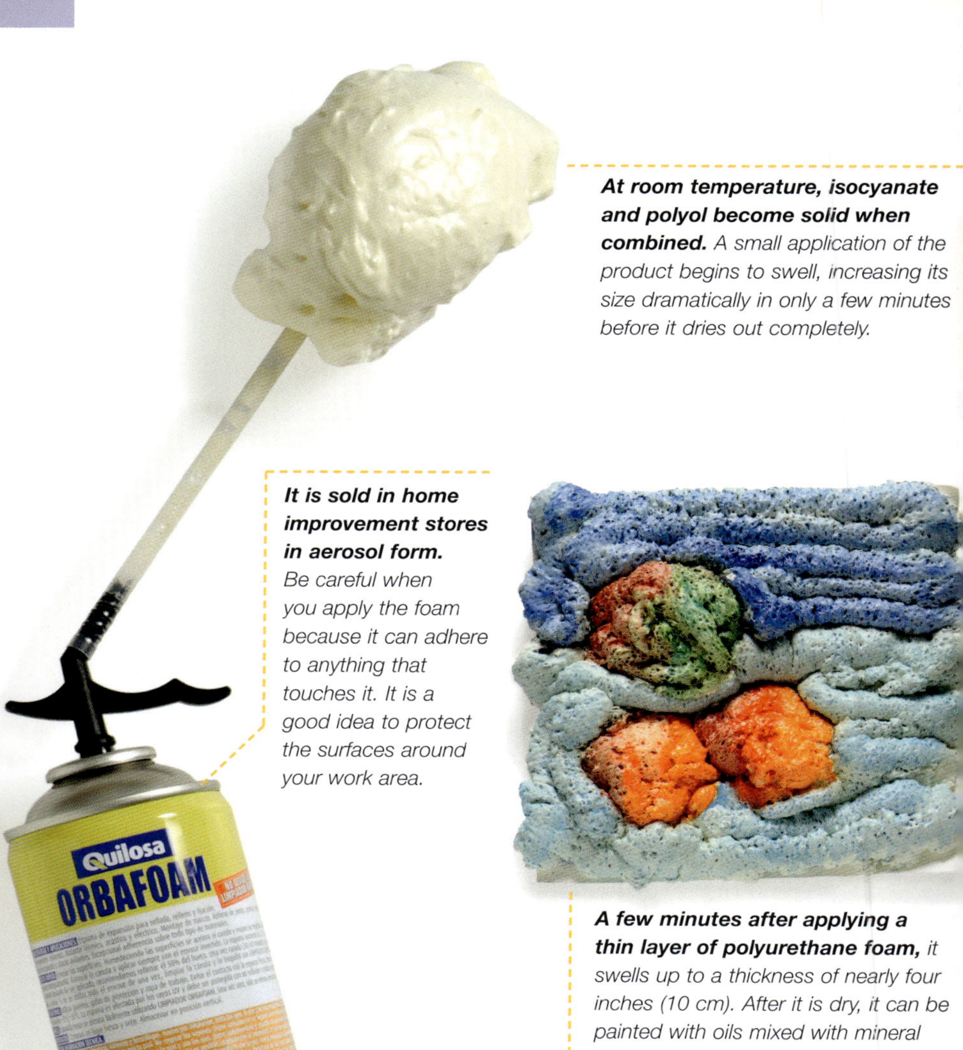

At room temperature, isocyanate and polyol become solid when combined. *A small application of the product begins to swell, increasing its size dramatically in only a few minutes before it dries out completely.*

It is sold in home improvement stores in aerosol form. *Be careful when you apply the foam because it can adhere to anything that touches it. It is a good idea to protect the surfaces around your work area.*

A few minutes after applying a thin layer of polyurethane foam, *it swells up to a thickness of nearly four inches (10 cm). After it is dry, it can be painted with oils mixed with mineral spirits.*

Plastic Foam

Polyurethane foam is a porous plastic material formed by an accumulation of bubbles. It is sometimes known as plastic foam. This synthetic plastic material, highly reticulated, and non-bondable, is sold in aerosol form in home improvement stores. It is created from the mixture of two chemical components: isocyanate and polyol, which are derived from combining petroleum and sugar. The reaction creates carbon dioxide, a gas that forms the bubbles.

Strong and Light

Once solidified, the foam is very strong. It is no coincidence that the expansion rate of the rigid foam is almost five times higher than that of cement. Therefore, it can easily be cut, carved with a craft knife, sanded, and painted with oils and acrylics. Other advantages of polyurethane foam are its light weight and the fact that is does not drip when being applied. This is why it is being used more and more by many artists wishing to create thee-dimensional effects in their paintings.

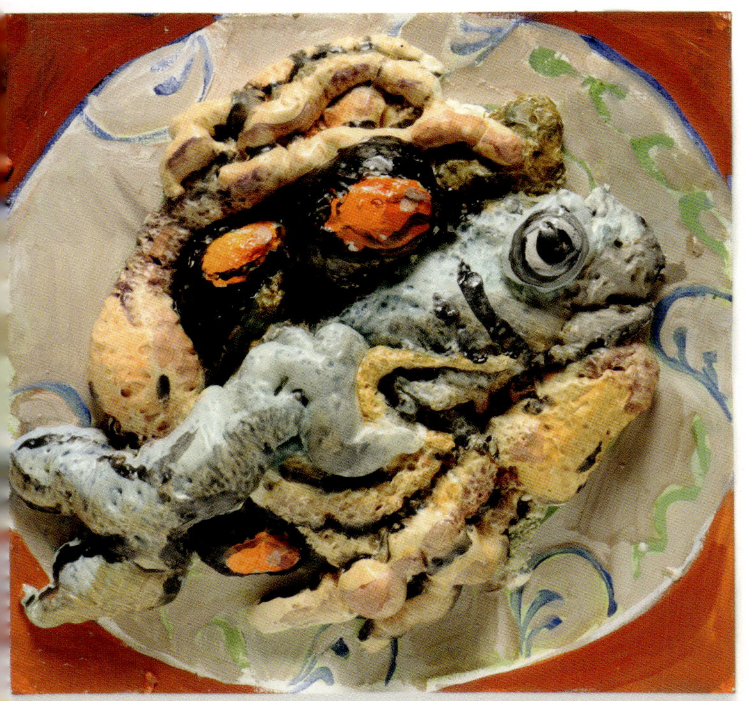

In time, you will be able to create actual forms and figures with the foam *and paint them with oils later. The whitish color of the foam favors the use of paint and keeps colors pure.*

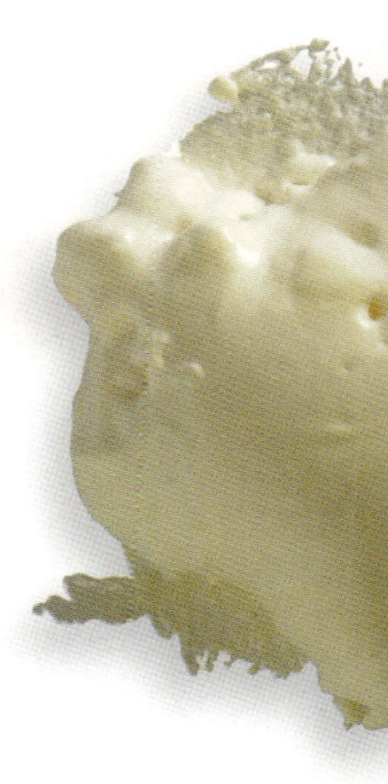

THE SUBJECT

Crackled Paint

Latex paint used for home interiors can be a useful material for creating cracked effects on the surface of the painting. If the layer of paint is thick and it is forced to dry fast, it can crack and break, producing an interesting texture that can be painted over with oil or acrylic paints.

Pour out the interior paint *and let it dry in the sun until cracks form.*

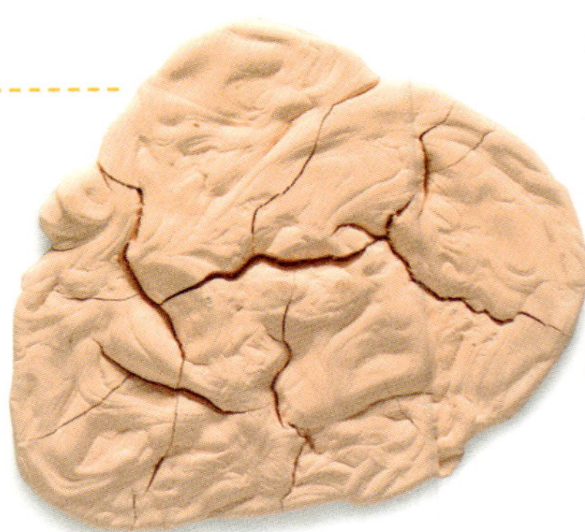

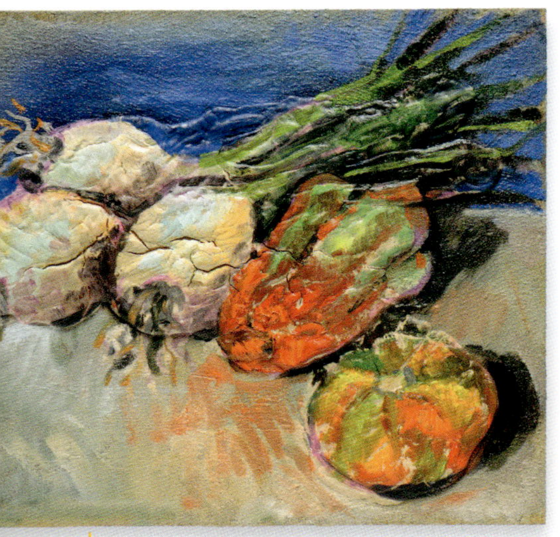

Latex paint poured directly from the can, *besides adding volume, provides a characteristic crackling effect that can be ideal for suggesting the texture of certain vegetables.*

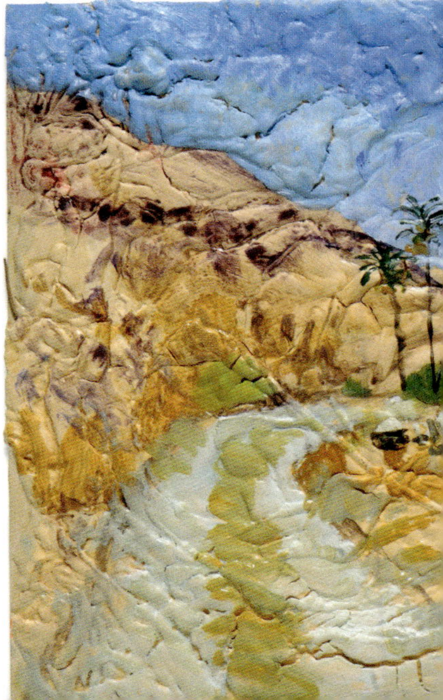

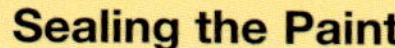

Pouring the Paint

Latex interior paint should be poured in large amounts over a hard surface—that is, canvas and brushes should not be used. Place a support flat on a table. The faster the paint dries, the greater the cracking will be, so the best thing to do is to put the support directly in the sun to dry. After a day, the thick layer of paint will be cracked and will show deep grooves. This provides an interesting background over which you can begin to paint.

Sealing the Paint

Before you begin to paint it is a good idea to cover the crackled paint with a light layer of gesso, latex, or varnish to seal any pores and make it stronger. This will also prevent new cracks from appearing after the painting is completed. When painting over this surface, your brush will glide easily. Try to keep the smooth oil or acrylic paint from getting into the cracks since the idea is to preserve them as part of the painting.

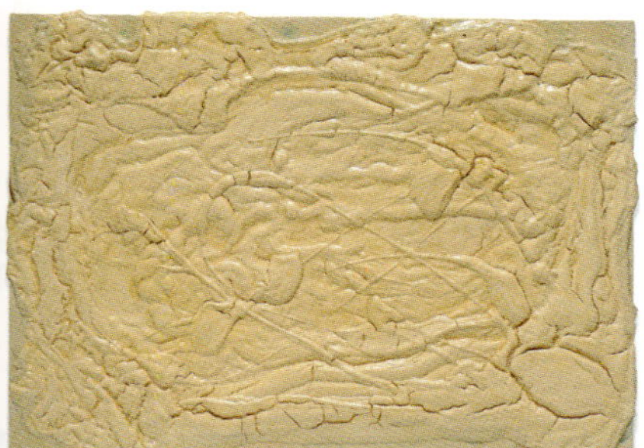

First, cover a wood board with a large amount of paint. *Cracks will appear after drying. Afterwards, seal the surface with a layer of aging varnish.*

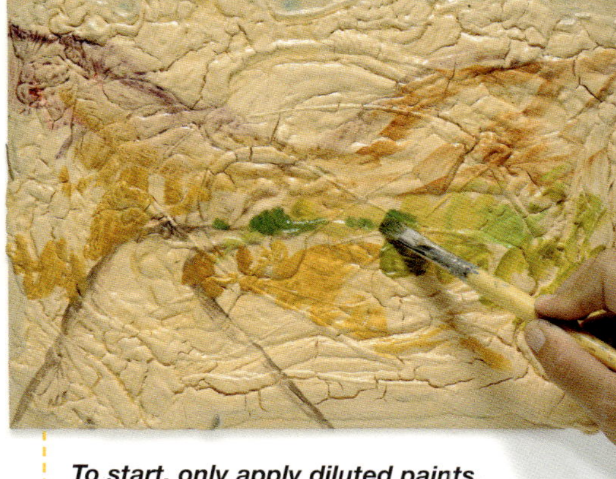

To start, only apply diluted paints. *This approach is not much different from painting over a typical smooth support.*

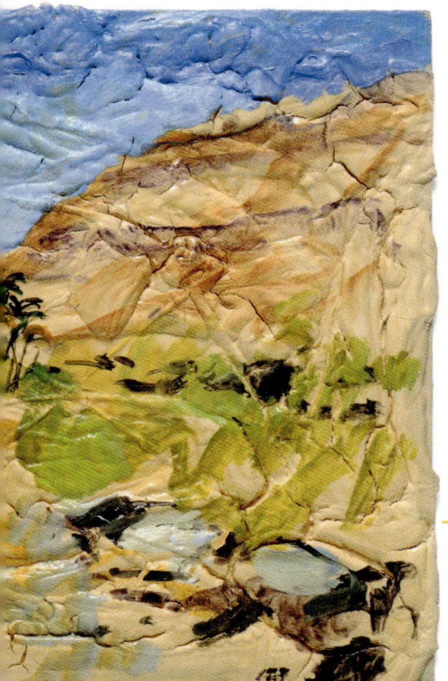

The finished work shows how the cracked texture *of the paint was used to define the rocky terrain that forms part of this landscape.*

Atypical Textures

We will finish by displaying a few atypical textures—a sample of ideas for those who like to experiment by combining different materials. These days in the art world almost anything goes so long as the final result adds visual interest to the work. It is important to avoid materials or substances that are too volatile, weak, or fragile, or that might detach from the painting when it dries.

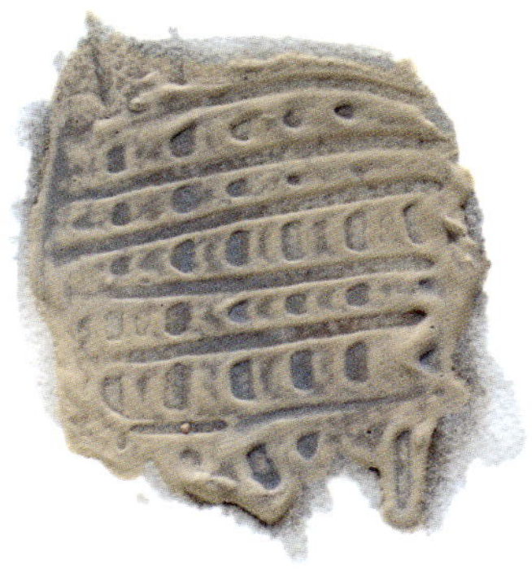

Create a sgraffito pattern in modeling paste. Then deposit the paint in the impressions.

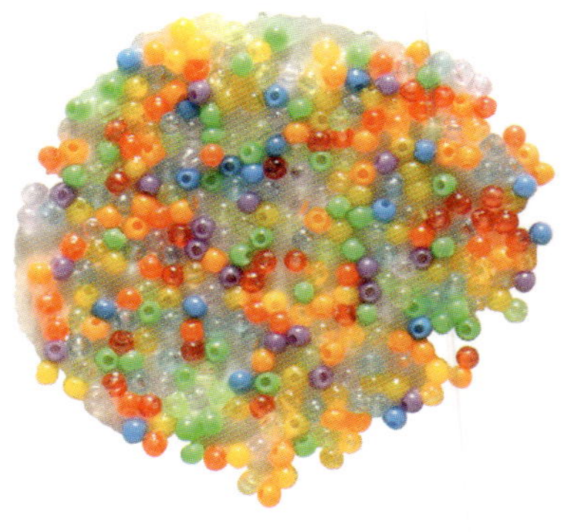

Cover the surface with colored beads that can be purchased in bulk in craft stores.

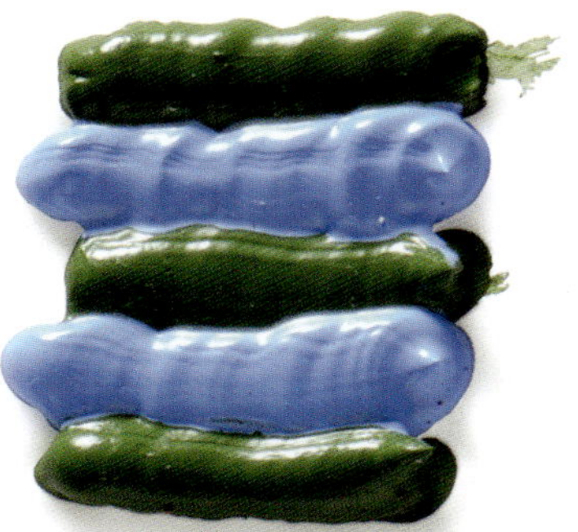

Alternate different colored stripes of very thick acrylic paint.

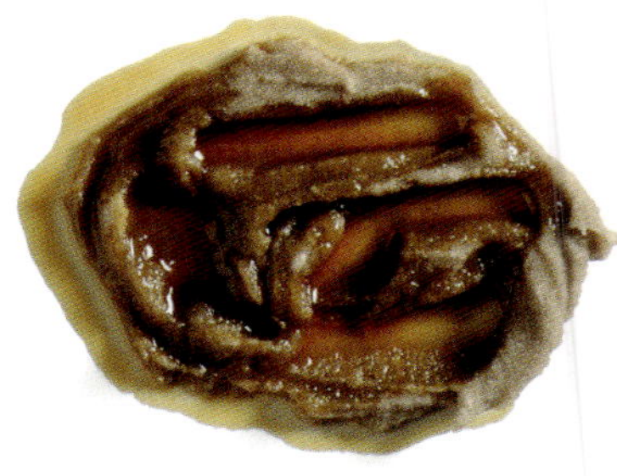

Create a few deep depressions in modeling paste that can then be filled with puddles of varnish.

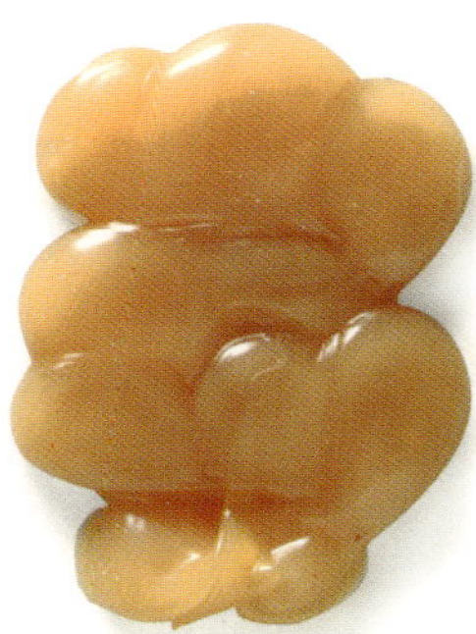

Dispense oleopasto directly from the tube to create a very pronounced texture in the form of round spirals.

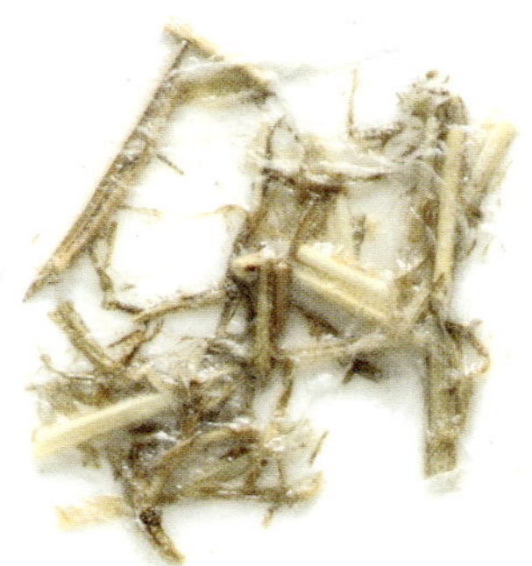

Glue a bit of straw on the support and cover it with a thin layer of tissue paper to create a glazed effect.

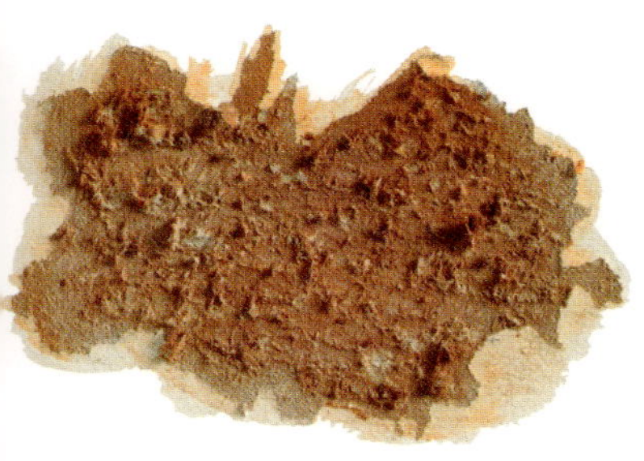

Use a craft knife to scrape a piece of wet cardboard until lumps are formed. Next, seal the texture with a layer of matte varnish.

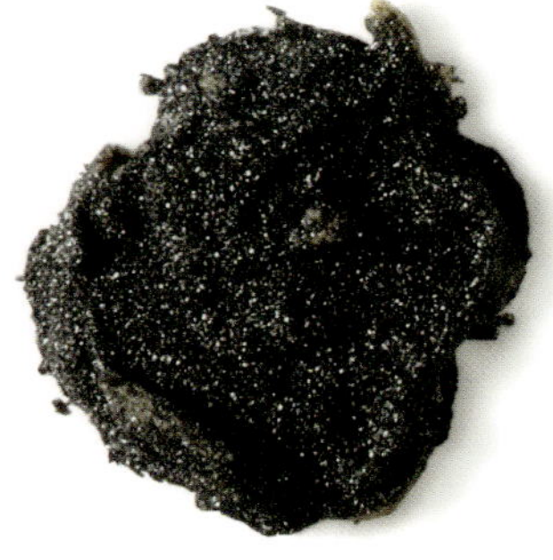

Use modeling paste to create volume. When it dries, wet it with latex or glue and then pour carborundum over it.

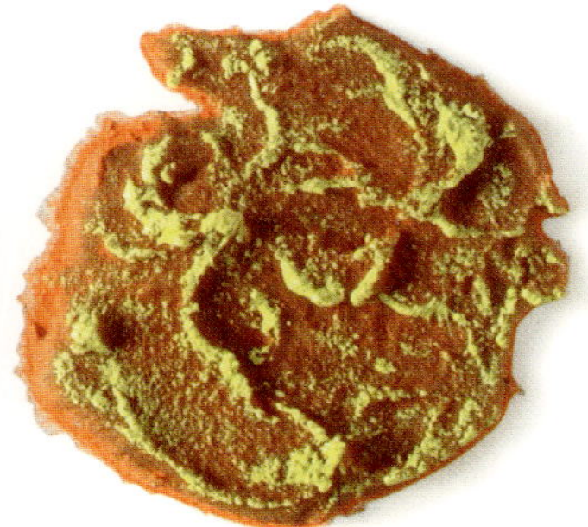

Apply oil paint over a texture created with modeling paste. Let it dry and then paint the high areas with a different color.

To obtain greater volume you can mix wax gel with fine sand. The drawback to this approach is its long drying time.

IN THE STYLE OF…

Alberto Burri (1915–1995)

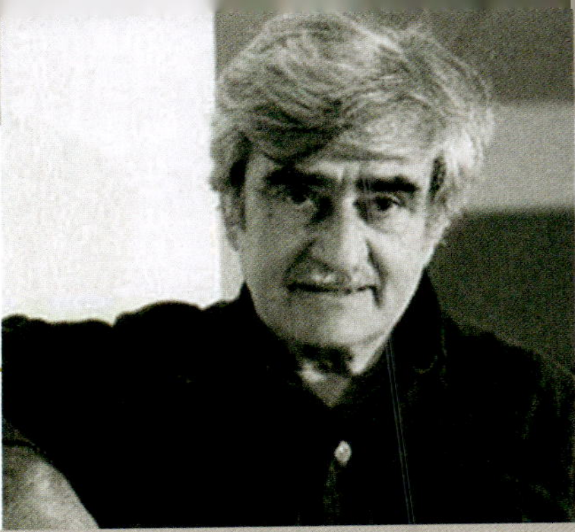

Burri incorporated into his paintings very unusual, everyday materials such as pumice, tar, and burlap.

Saco 5P *(1953)*
Beginning in 1950, Burri favored the collage and constructions with diverse materials. His first works painted on burlap bags date back to 1952. The bags were transformed into three-dimensional surfaces. In his approach, the texture and the chosen support became one and the same, and he used this raw base to apply the colors and to establish a dialogue between them. At the heart of Burri's paintings is the tense relationship between the constructed forms and the constructive dissolution of the form.

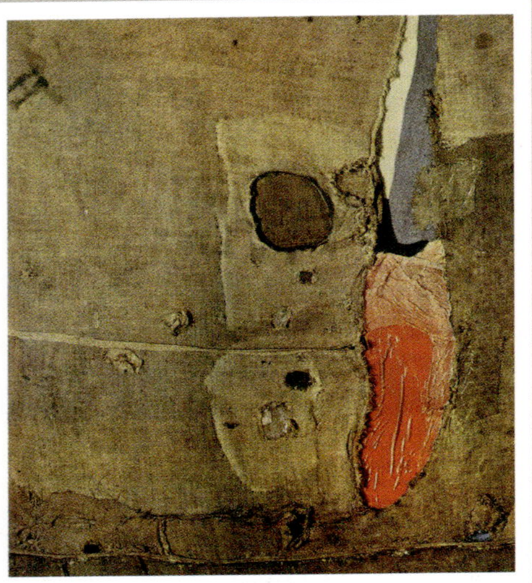

UNCONVENTIONA

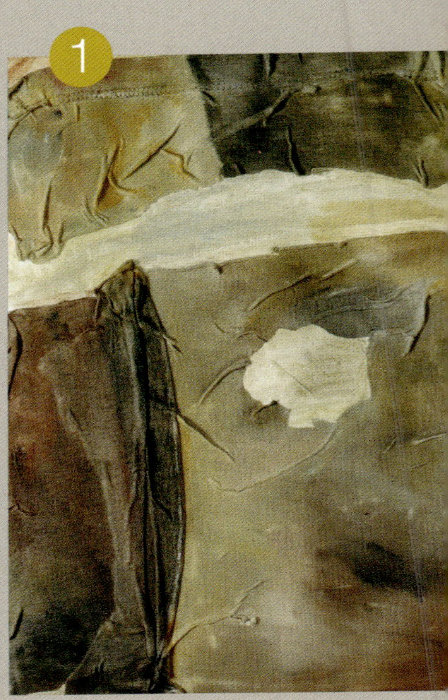

1. *An artist, as a creator of images, can benefit from Burri's ideas and incorporate them into his or her paintings. To this end, we have adhered wrinkled rags to the support, which are painted with gray and brown paint diluted with mineral spirits.*

This Italian painter began painting abstracts in 1949. He made paintings about materials, very close to the Informalist style, using very unconventional textures. He also used disposable materials that covered the entire support, or that became the support itself. His personal style was described as "poly materialist," although his work is related to European Tachisme, Abstract Expressionism, and Lyrical Abstraction.

EXTURES

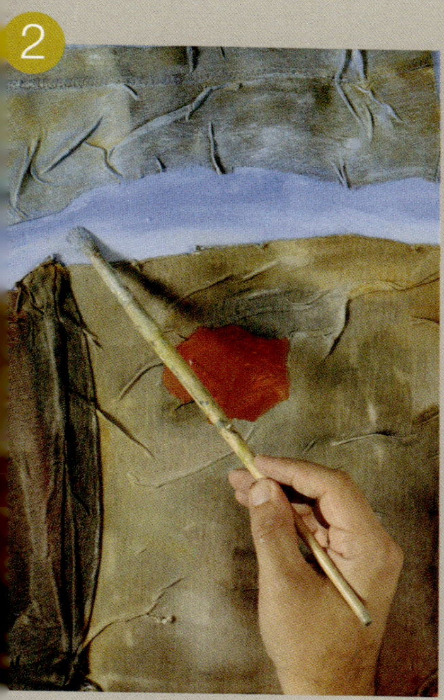

. We paint the upper part of the painting sing a mixture of blue and white oils, and he circle in the center, the area that is not overed with drapes, with red. We want to repare a textured background to paint a gurative subject.

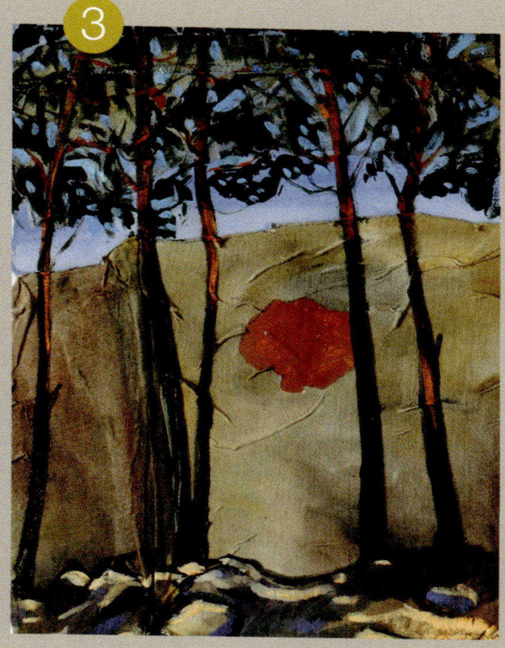

3. *Now we only need to paint the trees, which are in silhouette against the light in the foreground. The forms should be simple and the range of colors very restricted so they blend into the painting.*

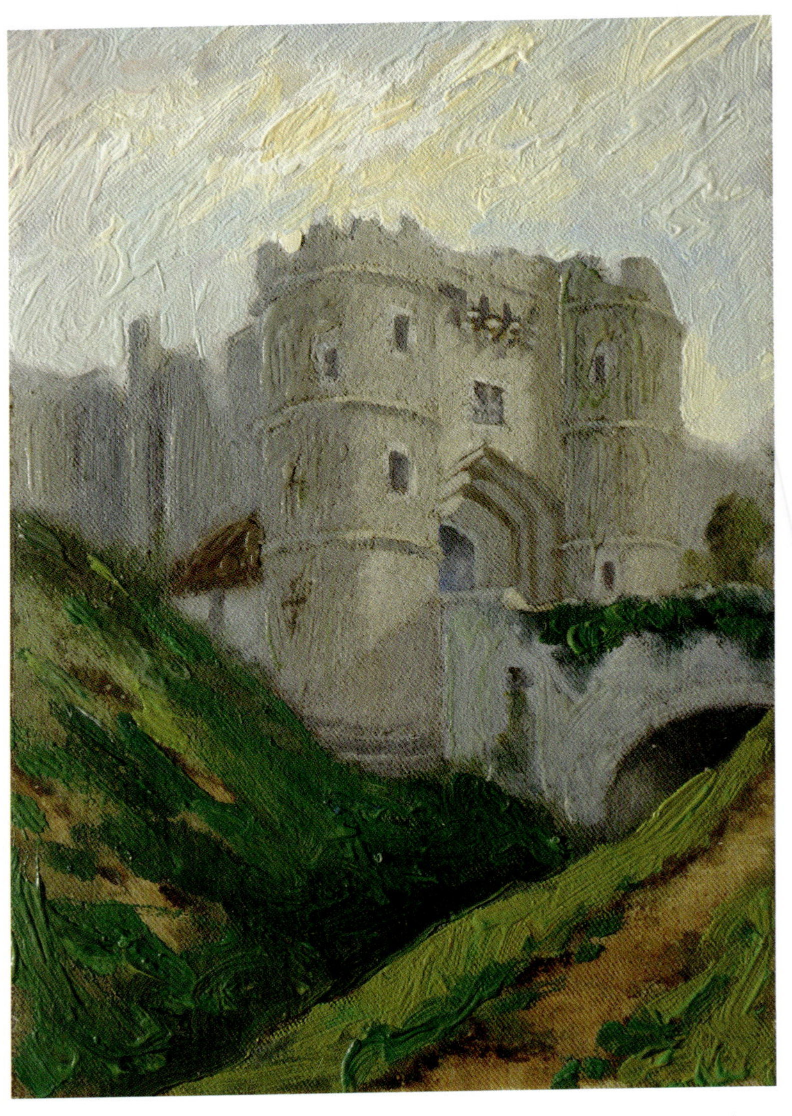

"Painting is a form of art that represents a sensed phenomenon on a plane... The artist transforms the conception of his experience into art. With continuous practice he learns to use the appropriate media. There are no set rules for it. The rules for a single work of art are formed during the process and through the personality of the artist, his own technique and the intended result."

Emil Nolde
Jahre de Kämft, 1959